RESOURCE BOOKS FOR TEACHERS

series editor

ALAN MALEY

STORYTELLING WITH CHILDREN

Andrew Wright

Oxford University Press 1995

Oxford University Press
Walton Street, Oxford OX2 6DP

Oxford New York
Athens Auckland Bangkok Bombay
Calcutta Cape Town Dar es Salaam Delhi
Florence Hong Kong Istanbul Karachi
Kuala Lumpur Madras Madrid Melbourne
Mexico City Nairobi Paris Singapore
Taipei Tokyo Toronto

and associated companies in
Berlin Ibadan

Oxford and *Oxford English* are trade marks of
Oxford University Press

ISBN 0 19 437202 2

© Oxford University Press 1995

Set by Wyvern Typesetting Ltd, Bristol

Printed in Hong Kong

Acknowledgements

I would like to thank the following people:

Irmgard Meyer for her support, generosity, and guidance over so many years.

David Betteridge, who has been an inspiration, a guide, and an 'ear' for all my stories.

Duncan Williamson for the privilege of meeting one of the greatest living storytellers. Duncan told me the story about the 'Little white cat' which he learnt from his aunt. The story in this book is not exactly as he told it and I hope he will not mind too much.

Jim Wingate for being a continual inspiration and source of ideas for activities to do with stories.

Mario Rinvolucri and John Morgan for their pioneering book *Once Upon a Time* (see Further Reading).

Eva Benkö for her detailed advice and very many suggestions which have been incorporated into various parts of the book. In particular, Eva contributed the lesson notes for 'Ma Liang', most of the ideas in the section 'Topics and stories', and many of the activities in the 'Store of 94 activities'!

Julia Dudás for her support and for the major contributions she made to the section 'Grammar and stories'.

Armida Scarpa for her lesson plan notes for 'Goldilocks'.

Aliza Irene Handler for her lesson plan notes for 'Father, son, and donkey'.

Leslie Cohen for her lesson plan notes for 'Nessy'.

Caroline Laidlaw for her ideas on chanting key lines, particularly for 'Ma Liang'.

Kathleen Powell and the children of Scuola Elementare Arcobaleno, Cailungo, Republic of San Marino (5th class) for their story submitted for the *JET* 21st Century Fairy Tale story competition 1993/4.

The children of Premontrei Primary School, Gödöllö, Hungary for their story 'The two little kittens'.

Nete Cleeman for her comments and suggestions on the manuscript.

Tom Wright for his determination, kindness, and patience in bringing me up to date with word processing for the typing of this manuscript.

Kay Bentley and an anonymous reviewer for their comments on the manuscript.

Julia Sallabank for her patience, encouragement, and editorial thoroughness.

Illustrations by Andrew Wright and Gwen Sallabank © Oxford University Press.

The publishers and author would like to thank the following for their kind permission to use or adapt extracts from copyright material. There are instances where we have been unable to trace or contact the copyright holder before our printing deadline. We apologize for this apparent negligence. If notified the publisher will be pleased to rectify any errors or omissions at the earliest opportunity.

Thomas Nelson and Sons Ltd. for 'Nessy' by Andrew Wright.

Canongate Books Ltd. for 'Strange animal' adapted from *Children of Wax: African Folk Tales* by Alexander McCall Smith, 1994.

Oxford University Press for an extract from *Oh No, I'm a Cat!* by Andrew Wright © Oxford University Press 1993.

Contents

6 More stories and ideas

7 Pages to copy

The author and series editor

Andrew Wright is an author, illustrator, teacher trainer, and storyteller. He has written 'Spellbinders', a series of six books for children at three levels for Oxford University Press. He has also written a number of books for teachers including *Games for Language Learning, 1000 + Pictures for Teachers to Copy*, and *Five Minute Activities* (with Penny Ur). He has worked in thirty countries as a teacher trainer, always concentrating on the application of practical and enjoyable activities in the classroom. In recent years he has worked with about 25,000 students as a storyteller and storymaker. Ten of his stories have been recorded by the BBC World Service, and ten have been broadcast on German Television and Thames Television in Britain. He is currently travelling as a storyteller and storymaker in schools in various countries and working on another book for this series, *Creating Stories with Children*.

Alan Maley worked for The British Council from 1962 to 1988, serving as English Language Officer in Yugoslavia, Ghana, Italy, France, and China, and as Regional Representative in South India (Madras). From 1988 to 1993 he was Director-General of the Bell Educational Trust, Cambridge. He is currently Senior Fellow in the Department of English Language and Literature of the National University of Singapore. He has written *Literature*, in this series, *Beyond Words, Sounds Interesting, Sounds Intriguing, Words, Variations on a Theme*, and *Drama Techniques in Language Learning* (all with Alan Duff), *The Mind's Eye* (with Françoise Grellet and Alan Duff), *Learning to Listen* and *Poem into Poem* (with Sandra Moulding), and *Short and Sweet*. He is also Series Editor for the Oxford Supplementary Skills series.

Foreword

'Once upon a time . . . ': magic words which open the door into new worlds where anything is possible because the normal rules of logic do not apply; worlds where children (of all ages) can let their imaginations loose in a framework of safe familiarity. And, once those words have been spoken, there must be few people who can resist the fascination as they are drawn deeper into the web of the story.

Clearly the power exerted by stories in the mother tongue has a similar potency in foreign language learning. They have a universal, archetypal appeal. Stories are comfortingly familiar; there is a 'grammar' of stories which can be followed by children even if they do not understand every word. They allow for the natural and enjoyable repetition of words and phrases. At the same time they offer opportunities for inventive variations through relating the stories to the learners' own lives and imaginations. They virtually solve the 'problem' of motivation at a stroke. And they offer multiple possibilities for spin-off activities involving visual, tactile, and dramatic elements.

Few would dispute these advantages, yet, until relatively recently, there has been very little concentrated work on storytelling in second language pedagogy. It is no exaggeration to say that Andrew Wright, through his workshops and storytelling sessions with children and teachers in many countries, has put storytelling on the map again. In this book he shares his long and rich experience of using stories in the teaching of English as a Foreign Language by offering systematic guidance to teachers who wish to incorporate stories into their practice. But, more than that, he shares with his readers his own enjoyment of the art of storytelling.

Alan Maley

Introduction

We all need stories for our minds as much as we need food for our bodies: we watch television, go to the cinema and theatre, read books, and exchange stories with our friends. Stories are particularly important in the lives of our children: stories help children to understand their world and to share it with others. Children's hunger for stories is constant. Every time they enter your classroom they enter with a need for stories.

Who is this book for?

Children

In this book, the activities described have been used with children aged seven to fourteen with between six months and three years of English. This is a very wide range of experience and potential learning development. Furthermore, in my experience the difference between one class and another, even of the same age and in the same school, can be enormous. So much depends on whether English is part of the children's lives in their society, how enthusiastic and informed their parents are about English, how naturally English is used by the teacher in the normal life of the class, and last but not least, how free the children feel to 'have a go' in English.

Children can be helped to understand quite complex stories in language well above their own active command. *It is what we expect the children to do which determines the proficiency level required, not the story itself.*

Teachers

This book is for teachers who believe in the enormous importance of stories in the daily lives of their children and in the English lesson, and who would like a few pointers and examples in order to make stories central to their teaching. Don't worry if you are not very experienced in using stories or if you feel that your own English is not very good—I have tried to make the explanations easy to follow.

Why stories?

Stories, which rely so much on words, offer a major and constant source of language experience for children. Stories are motivating, rich in language experience, and inexpensive! Surely, stories should be a central part of the work of all primary teachers whether they are teaching the mother tongue or a foreign language.

Here are some of the most important reasons why stories should play a central role in teaching a foreign language to children.

Motivation

Children have a constant need for stories and they will always be willing to listen or to read, if the right moment is chosen.

Meaning

Children want to find meaning in stories, so they listen with a purpose. If they find meaning they are rewarded through their ability to understand, and are motivated to try to improve their ability to understand even more. This is in contrast to so many activities in foreign language learning, which have little or no intrinsic interest or value for children.

Fluency

Listening and reading fluency

In conversations with native speakers the most important ability is to be able to understand a sustained flow of the foreign language in which there are words which are *new* to the listener. The ability to do this can only be built up by practice.

Listening and reading fluency is based on:
- a positive attitude to not understanding everything
- the skills of searching for meaning, predicting, and guessing.

Children are expert at doing this in their own language but it takes time and encouragement for them to build up these skills and attitudes in the foreign language. If you feel that you are not fluent in English that is partly because your teachers did not give you enough time and encouragement!

Speaking and writing fluency

Fluency in speaking is not only essential in conversation but is, for many people, the spearhead of how they learn. Fluency is based on a positive attitude to 'having a go' with the language one knows and not being afraid of making mistakes. It is also based on the skill of constructing meaning with limited language. Some people learn best by 'having a go' when they have nothing to fear or be anxious about; all their intelligence and creativity is employed to the full. I am sure that for many children this is the natural way to learn. This means that the teacher must give more importance to what the child achieves than to the mistakes he or she might make. It also means that the teacher must encourage situations in which the child can be fluent and can 'have a go'. Stories offer a perfect diet for the buildup of fluency in all four skills.

Language awareness

Stories help children become aware of the general 'feel' and sound of the foreign language. Stories also introduce children to language items and sentence constructions without their necessarily having to use them productively. They can build up a reservoir of language in this way. When the time comes to move the language items into their productive control, it is no great problem because the language is not new to them.

An obvious example of a language point introduced and made familiar through stories before the children are expected to use it fluently themselves is the simple past tense.

Stimulus for speaking and writing

The experience of the story encourages responses through speaking and writing. It is natural to express our likes and dislikes and to exchange ideas and associations related to stories we hear or read. In this way stories can be part of a set of related activities.

Communication

Listening and reading stories and responding to them through speaking and writing, drama, music, and art develop a sense of being and having an audience and of sharing and collaborating. Learning a language is useless if we do not know how to communicate—how to listen to others and how to speak and write so that listeners and readers will want to listen and read and be able to understand. Story sharing builds up this crucial sense of awareness of others.

General curriculum

Most stories can be used to develop the children's powers of
awareness, analysis, and expression, as well as relating to other
aspects of the curriculum such as cultural and social studies,
geography, history, mathematics, and science
(see Chapter 4).

Danger! Story health warning!

If the teacher uses stories merely to introduce and practise
grammar or particular lexical areas or functions, the children
may lose their faith in the teacher and what she or he means by
the word 'story'. When focusing on features of the language be
careful not to lose the magic of the story altogether!

How to use this book

How this book is organized

1 How to choose, tell, and read stories aloud

In order for children to be able to respond to stories they must
hear them or read them. The book begins by giving suggestions
on choosing, reading, and telling stories.

2 A store of 94 activities

In recent years an enormous number of activities associated with
the use of stories in language development has been built up.
This section of the book summarizes many of these activities.
The activities are arranged roughly according to when you might
want to use them and what your broad purpose might be.

3 Stories and lesson plans

In this section there are a number of stories and lesson plans showing how the activities from the previous section might be used. You must adapt these plans to suit each of your classes. One way is to take a lesson plan which I have used for one story and use it with another story.

Most of the stories have cartoon picture strips or worksheets to help you use them in class.

4 Topics and stories

The activities in this section place their emphasis on the potential link between stories and the broader primary curriculum. They are a sequence of activities which you can do with the story given. If you do the whole sequence it will take you a long time! You must select according to your children's needs and interests.

5 Grammar and stories

In this section the activities focus on particular features of the language which you might like the children to concentrate on or become aware of.

6 More stories and ideas

In this section there are seventeen stories plus brief notes on classroom activities. I hope you will find these stories and ideas useful in spite of their brevity.

7 Pages to copy

These pages contain pictures which are generally useful and relate to all the stories, for example, tips on drawing characters and other items.

Further reading

A brief, annotated list of publications you might like to follow up.

How each activity is organized

Level

The level is based on what the children are expected to *do* in the activity and not on the complexity of the language in the story. This is a most important principle and is often confused when teachers are assessing a story. For example, in 6.9, 'Skiing accident', it is probably an elementary-level task for children to listen to the story and then to express an opinion about the truth of it. But it would be a pre-intermediate or even higher task for the children to write their own 'true or false' story. In Chapter 4 there is an activity (4.9, 'Mice can . . . ') which elementary children can do if it is kept to boasting: *I can run very fast*. But it becomes a pre-intermediate task if we ask them to say *I can run faster than you*. The most extreme example of level being determined by activity and not by the story itself is Armida Scarpa's lesson plans for 'Goldilocks', 3.10, categorized in this book as 'elementary' but used by Armida with beginners.

In my own work as a storyteller I frequently tell stories to children which might be judged as far too difficult for them. Usually I am quite satisfied if the children feel that they have understood and enjoyed most of the story.

Beginners

From children with little or no knowledge of English to those who recognize and might be able to use the English words for colours, numbers, and basic vocabulary such as family, animals, food, *I am/you are*, *there is/there are*, *can*, *I like/don't like*, and classroom commands such as *stand up*, *sit down*, *open your books*. Present simple and continuous tenses only.

Their active use of this language will be very limited. And the children's response will often be limited to listening and acting or listening and arranging sentence cards, etc. However, there is no reason why children at any level should not encounter language beyond that which they are currently learning for active use, provided that it does not confuse them or prevent them from enjoying the story and the activity you are asking them to do.

Note: I have not provided any suggestions for helping children whose own mother tongue is not based on Roman script.

Elementary

These children are able to use English more actively, and to make simple sentences and questions. They will have a wider range of vocabulary: for example, clothes, shops, parts of the body, verbs for daily routines, and telling the time in English (if they know it in their own language).

Pre-intermediate

These children will be more capable of recognizing sentence patterns and more willing to 'have a go' at generating language of their own. They are ready to learn structures such as the past simple and past continuous, comparatives, possibly *going to*, and functions such as obligation, requests, or making suggestions.

Age

Experience shows that it is not easy to know what is going to appeal to different ages of children. Sometimes fourteen-year-olds will happily accept a story written for much younger children. Sometimes a class of very young children will accept a most serious story meant for adults. The ages given in the activities can only be rough guides!

Time

A rough guide only.

Language

The language features and skills which are practised in the activity.

Materials

Any materials you need to get hold of in advance in order to do the activity.

Preparation

What you need to do before the lesson begins.

In class

A step-by-step guide to what you do in class. It is important that you adjust this to the needs of your children. For example, these activities have not been designed to *introduce* new language points, and you should not rely on them to provide the only experience the children need of English.

Follow-up(s)

Examples of further activities which relate to either the language points or the topic of the main activity.

1 How to choose, tell, and read stories aloud

Telling and reading stories to children is a central part of classroom life. This section of the book is about how to choose, tell, and read aloud as well as possible. Of course, some people are 'born' storytellers, but that applies to every ability we have. The fact is that we can all improve our storytelling and story reading, and that is what matters.

Telling or reading aloud?

We need both salt and pepper in our cooking. Why should we want to say that one is better than the other? Telling and reading aloud both have their strong points.

Reading aloud

Good points

1 You don't have to learn the story.

2 You don't have to worry about making mistakes in English.

3 If you read the story then the children will always hear exactly the same text and this will help them to predict what is to come.

4 It demonstrates that books are a source of interesting ideas and so encourages reading.

5 The children can, perhaps, borrow the book afterwards.

6 Pictures in the book help the children's understanding.

Not so good points

1 You must be careful not to read too quickly because written texts are usually very precise, economical, and unrepetitive, and that makes listening to them rather difficult.

2 It is easy to 'bury yourself' in a book and forget the listeners! See the tips on page 21.

Telling

Good points

1 The children feel that you are giving them something very personal. The story is yours; it is not coming out of a book.

2 Children, these days, are rarely used to the experience of hearing someone tell a story and it can have a powerful effect on them.

3 It is often easier to understand a story being told than one which is read aloud:
- it is natural to repeat oneself when speaking;
- you can see the children's faces and bodies and respond to their lack of comprehension, their joy, and their immediate concerns more readily;
- you can make use of your body more effectively to heighten meaning;
- you can use the language you know the children know.

Not so good points

1 You must learn the story well enough to tell it without the book (see the tips on page 15).

2 You might make some mistakes in your English.

Your English and the telling of stories

One of the best ways of improving your English is to learn stories—to internalize a ten-minute flow of English. Traditional teaching did not develop fluency. Oral fluency needs time, opportunity, and encouragement to develop, and that applies to you as well as to the children (see page 6). If you learn a story you have a real purpose—to communicate it to the children. And how lucky you are because children are an appreciative and kindly audience.

So, if your English is not very fluent and accurate then that is an excellent reason for telling stories to children!

Choosing a story

Choose a story:
- which will engage the children within the first few lines (note that children often accept and like a story in the foreign language they might feel was childish in their own language)

- which you like
- which you feel is appropriate for the children
- which the children will understand well enough to enjoy
- which offers the children a rich experience of language
- which does not have long descriptive passages
- which is right for the occasion and in its relation with other things you are doing with the children
- which you feel you can tell well.

Remembering a story

There are various ways of remembering stories, and you must find the way most appropriate to you.

It is difficult to remember a written story word for word, like an actor—and in any case, it seems rather artificial when it is done like this. Why try to do it? Concentrate on learning the gist of the story rather than every detail of it.

Here are some techniques:
- read the story or listen to it a few times and then try to retell it on to a tape or to a friend
- explicitly select the key points, write them down, perhaps in bubbles as in the example here for 3.8, 'Ma Liang'.

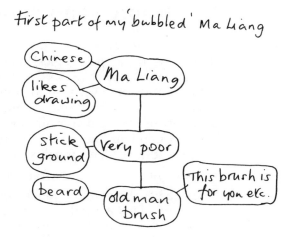

First part of my 'bubbled' Ma Liang

This is the technique that I use. Note how I have added extra details to the bubbles but if I forget them I know that I can still tell the story. It is important to make each bubbled story look different because it will then be easier to remember visually. It is the actual making of the bubbled story which helps to get it into the memory. Later the bubbled story acts as a useful and rapid mnemonic.

- Instead of putting the key points in bubbles, you might prefer simply to write out the key points. This is called a story skeleton (see Morgan and Rinvolucri, *Once Upon a Time—* details in Further Reading).
- See the story as a film in your imagination and let your telling of the story be guided by that inner vision.
- You could remember a dramatic or verbal rhythm in the story. (I think I am right in saying that the great West Indian storyteller, Grace Hallworth, learns her stories in this way.)
- Remember the personalities of the characters and this will remind you of the story. (Duncan Williamson, one of whose many stories is on page 92 (3.6 'The little white cat'), told me this is what he does.)

Whatever technique you use, it is probably best not to tell it dramatically the first time. Find a friend who will listen to you and try it on them. Warn them that you will just concentrate on getting the gist of the story right. Once you are confident that you can remember the basic story, you can concentrate on expressing what you feel about the story in future tellings. The more often you tell the story, the more you will feel 'at home' with it. Do not expect to tell it brilliantly the first time. Furthermore, the more stories you learn, the easier it is to learn new ones.

Just before you tell or read the story

I am referring here to the craft of storytelling and story reading rather than to the pedagogical preparation, which is discussed in a later section (see pages 28–39 and 73). Half the success of a story depends on what you do before you begin! The children must be in the right 'frame of mind' for a story. If they think it is all part of the normal lesson they will be in their 'normal' frame of mind and not in their 'story' frame of mind, and you will probably not have much success.

So they must be in a story frame of mind!

- Try to get the children much nearer to you than is normally the case. This is partly because it is important for them to see you (and your book if you are using one), but it is also because it changes the relationship between you and them and each other. They know they are going to share something.
Younger children can be asked to sit on the floor around your feet.
- If at all possible change the seating before the story is told. I always try to do this before the children come into the class. My preferred arrangement is a U-shape of chairs with a U-shape of tables immediately behind. Some children sit on the chairs and some children sit on the edges of the tables.

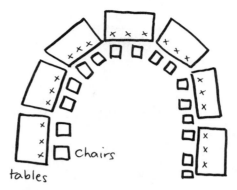

— If you cannot change the arrangement of tables and chairs,
then try to find some other way of helping the children to feel
that something special is going to happen (rather than merely
saying so). Children are so used to hearing you talk; they just
assume it is going to be what they have had before. Some
teachers always sit on their table or stand in a particular part
of the room when they are going to tell a story and never do
this at any other time.

— Some teachers have a 'story bag' (which might be just an
ordinary plastic bag) which they only have to hold up for the
children to get into their 'story frame of mind'. Other teachers
often make use of a friendly puppet. Others might always wear
a particular hat or coat.

— You can put some music on—always use the same music and
then the children will know and get themselves ready.

— Once, in a noisy class, I wrote on the board *I'd like to tell you
a story*. Then I sat down on a chair in an open space at the
front of the children and waited. I didn't have to ask them to
be quiet. You might write *A story for you* or just *Story time*.

— Perhaps have a regular time for your storytelling or story
reading, and the time will put them into the right frame of
mind.

— For particular stories you might display a picture before you
begin, or an object like an old umbrella, or a basket with food

in it for 3.7, 'Little Red Riding Hood'. An antique doll can be used to tell the story of her times. A Cinderella puppet can tell the Cinderella story.

Different ways of beginning

- Talk with the children about their experience of what you know will be a central topic of the story. For example, *Hairy Tree Man*, a story in my 'Spellbinders' series from Oxford University Press, is about brother and sister relationships. One way of beginning the story would be to ask the children about their relationships with brothers and sisters.
- Begin with an explicit introduction to the story: for example, 'I'm going to tell you a story about a little white cat'. Then you can tell them the 'Little white cat' story (3.6, page 92).
- Begin without any preparation at all, directly with the first line of the story, or with *Once upon a time*.
- Don't begin until you have everyone's attention and total silence—unless you are confident that the sheer power of your telling is going to quieten them down.

Your manner

You must tell stories in your own way and that way must be a normal part of you. Grace Hallworth, the West Indian storyteller, is quiet and dignified as a person and as a storyteller she is just the same. Duncan Williamson, the Scottish storyteller, is full of fun in normal conversation and is just the same in his storytelling. I would say, heighten slightly what you are and see everything about yourself positively. If you are a quiet sort of person, then choose the stories you like and tell them quietly!

But I do think that, whatever kind of personality you have, you must give yourself totally to your story and to your listeners if you want to get back a strong quality of listening and appreciation from them. Many people who are not confident as storytellers don't want to risk failure, so they don't really give themselves and then they get a feeble response because of it.

Your voice

The potential variety of the human voice includes: pitch, volume, rhythm, softness/harshness, pace, and pause. Making use of this variety depends on the story, the personality of the teller, and the listeners. Of course, a dramatic use of the full variety of all of these qualities would often be inappropriate. On the other hand, many people do not make sufficient use of this potential richness, and produce a monotone.

You have probably not got the time to go on a course in voice training! On the other hand, there are some basic things that we can all do:

- Sit or stand so that you can breathe easily—don't be 'all hunched up'.
- Keep breathing while talking so you don't become breathless.
- Speak loudly enough for the children at the back to hear easily, but not by using a harsh 'teacher's voice' designed to cut through school corridors and across school playgrounds.
- Adopt a different voice for the narrator and for each of the characters. Make these voices very different: high/low, soft/harsh.
  A simple experiment—try saying a very ordinary sentence so that it sounds like the start of an amazing story. For example, *I got up this morning and opened the curtain.*
  A second experiment—try saying the sentence in several moods: happily, unhappily, wickedly, innocently, in a thoughtful way, in a casual way, in a frightened way.
- Pace and pause: the pause is one of the most powerful of all qualities in storytelling and reading. The listeners have to become active in order to fill it in—they try to predict what you will say next. It is one of the most vital elements in dramatic storytelling. Use it at key moments.
- Remember that in English we tend to stress the important words in a sentence. This helps to convey meaning.

The language

Be prepared to pre-teach important words and phrases which are an intrinsic part of the story. They might be important for the meaning of the story (for example, *chimney sweep* is an important pair of words in 3.6, 'The little white cat'), or they might be important for their play on words and sounds (for example, the repetition of *dark, dark,* in 3.2, 'In a dark, dark, town', page 78).

Even simple words can be spoken as if they are important. Speak slowly and enjoy the sound of the words you say. Of course, this is easier to do in one's mother tongue than in a foreign language. A feeling of rhythm and rhyme almost certainly helps people to learn and remember. Stories in verse are loved and effective.

Make sure you are confident of how to begin and finish the story. Many storytellers say that you should learn the first and the last lines by heart. Personally, I do this with some stories, but with others I like to slide the listeners into the story before they know they are in it.

Make the story yours and theirs. You might pause in the story to say to a child, if it is true, *You've been to China, haven't you, Hans?* Omit, add, change, and emphasize if you have a good reason. But be careful—the great traditional stories have stood the test of time.

Your body and face

It is probably true that we communicate as much or more through our bodily and facial movement than we do by the words we use. We can move quickly or slowly, jerkily or smoothly, with grand gestures, or with minor movements of our eyebrows. We can remain seated or we can move and act out not only the players within our story but even inanimate objects! The way we make use of this potential depends on our nature and on the nature of the story and the listeners.

Just as, in general, less experienced storytellers employ a monotonous voice, so they also fail to use the full potential of their body for communication. Indeed, they may use their body and face to communicate their primary concern, their own anxiety, rather than the quality of the story! Here are some tips.

- If you are telling a story rather than reading aloud from a book, you can easily move like Little Red Riding Hood as she picks the flowers (see 3.7, page 96), or you can hold up one of your hands in front of your face and slowly look round it with a wicked smile to represent the wolf. As you creep into the dark cave with the little Indian boy (3.4, page 84) you can hold out your hands and pretend to be putting them down on the ground very, very slowly and you can switch your eyes from side to side as if searching the darkness.
- Involve the children, for example, as you lift the axe off the paper in the 'Ma Liang' story (3.8, page 103), walk across to a child and pretend to give it to him or her.
- Very often I find that I begin to make the action with my body a split second before I refer to it. So, for example, I might hold up my hand to my ear and switch my eyes to and fro just a moment before I say, 'He listened'.
- Make your movements simple, slow, and never apologetic! I think body movements in storytelling should be just a little slower and bigger than you would do them in normal conversation. Give the children time to appreciate your movements and time to feel how they contribute to the

meaning of the story. We are gripped by stories and storytellers because we feel they really know what they are doing and saying; your storytelling must be clear and simple and not fleeting and confusing like normal life. But I say, 'I think', because we must all find our own way of telling.

- Look at people as you tell the story. Don't just scan their faces so that you can claim you were looking, but really look. It doesn't do any harm to look at one particular child for several moments as you tell the story. Other children feel that you are concentrating on them and not just on the story.

Interruptions

One child might chatter to a neighbour. The school caretaker might knock at the door. Someone might drop a book. What do you do?

Children not paying attention

- If it is several children, it may be that you are not being dramatic enough. Liven things up. Move around as you tell the story.
- Involve the children, for example, by asking them what they would do in the situation in the story.
- If one child is chattering then go and stand very near to him or her as you tell the story or even tell the story directly to him or her.

School caretaker knocking at the door

Don't try to compete! Quietly ask someone to see who it is and deal with it in the normal way.

Dropping of a book

- Pause, show no expression of annoyance, perhaps pick up the book yourself, and then carry on.
- Make a joke out of it, perhaps related to the story.

The important thing is not to break the magic spell. You have lifted the children off the ground and you are holding them there. Avoid returning, however momentarily, to your normal teaching voice and manner. That would jolt them off the magic carpet and out of their 'story frame of mind'.

Don't use the cancellation of a storytelling as a punishment.

Extra tips on reading from a book

- Read the story beforehand and get to know it and how to read it with some sense of drama. Also make sure you can pronounce all the words and know what they mean.

- Don't speak into the book. As general guidance, read the story to the children at the back of the group.
- Read slowly and with a more dramatic quality than in normal speech.
- Stop to comment, or to invite comments, quite often.
- Look up and try to make eye contact. Check that the whole group is with you.
- Stop to show the pictures and make sure all the children can see them.
- Have your finger ready to open the next page.
- Don't read for longer than about ten minutes (less for younger children).

Children telling and reading aloud

A few teachers might like to develop the children's storytelling skills along the lines given in the notes above. However, it would be very time-consuming and difficult to do so with a large class. Nevertheless, just being able to tell a story, even if it is not done dramatically, is very worthwhile in terms of confidence and the development of fluency.

Children reading aloud

It is highly questionable whether it is useful for children to read aloud. If it is to be done then at least let each child choose the text they are going to read, check with you that they understand it, practise it, and only then read it. But what about the rest of the class as the single child reads? Clearly they are going to fall asleep or cause trouble unless they are given something to do. So, for example, you might request that every child has to add something untrue to the text that they read out which the others have to find.

You can ask the children to make a class recording of a story with a new part added each day by a different child.

For other examples of reading activities, see 2.92, 'Reading race', 3.12, 'Strange animal', and 5.2, 'Half sentences'.

Choral reading

Choral reading is unfashionable but offers many benefits. For example, all the children speak and shy children do not feel exposed.

Here are some suggestions for organizing choral reading:

- Discuss the meaning of each line of the text and the feeling which the children need to express.
- Record and play back to the children their texts. Above all, contrast their improved renderings with earlier ones.
- Look for a variety of voices: all the children; half the children followed by the other half; a narrator or group of narrators, with other groups of children taking the part of one of the protagonists; your voice.
- Use background music or even pre-recorded natural noises.
- Use clapping or tapping to keep a rhythm going.
- Use voice training exercises which help the children to get used to speaking with the full range of their voices. Ask the children to read : slowly, quickly, quietly, quickly, sadly, happily, angrily, wearily. They can be asked to read the text as if it were a love story, horror story, adventure story, or a funny story. You can direct this by writing these words on different cards and showing them the cards as they read.
- Pyramid reading: the whole class reads the first sentence loudly, then the first sentence again quietly, and the second sentence loudly; then the first and second sentences quietly, and the third line loudly—i.e. each time reading an extra sentence, with only the last one read loudly, until the whole text has been read.
- Radio reading: the whole class reads chorally. When you clap they immediately read silently but with their lips moving. When you clap again they say the lines aloud again— together—you hope!

A checklist for the craft of your storytelling

Question   **Yes No**

1 Were the children engaged?
2 Did they understand enough to enjoy it?
3 Did they all hear me?
4 Did I forget any key bits?
5 Did I put all my energy into it?
6 Did I use enough variety of voice?
7 Did I use my body enough?
8 Did I look up and involve them enough?

Comments

_____

_____

2 A store of 94 activities

In this chapter I describe some of the most useful activities which can be applied to nearly all stories. I also give some broad reasons for using them. In the next chapter, 'Stories and lesson plans', I give examples of how some of these activities can be sequenced to provide one or two lessons based on particular stories.

Choosing activities

What do you want the activity for? To help the children to understand 'new' language? To give them an opportunity to express their feelings about the story? You should have a good reason for your choice. Your next decision is: Do you want to use the activities before, during, or after the story? If so, why?

Also remember that you can do an activity before, during, or after the second, third, or fourth telling of a story. Note that some of the activities listed here under 'during' are best done during the second or third telling rather than the first.

Level

Many of the activities can be used at a variety of learner ages and language levels. Only you, the teacher, can decide which activities are appropriate for your children. All of the activities are suitable (or adaptable) for all levels and age groups, unless a particular level is given.

Fluency

In many of the activities I suggest that you discuss aspects of the story and the children's experience of it, and that the children retell the story. I believe that children should be encouraged to attempt to express their ideas, opinions, and experiences from the very early days of language learning even if they can only use single words or short phrases. If they make mistakes in these 'sharing' moments, concentrate on what they are trying and managing to say rather than on the mistakes. It is the *process* we are concerned with, not just the final product.

At other times you might encourage the children to use their mother tongue to respond to the story and in this way keep up a high level of involvement. In other words, it is possible for any level of learner to engage in discussion. Of course, the age of the child is another factor. My own experience of children, however, suggests that children of almost any age can contribute experiences, ideas, and feelings about anything if you relate it to their lives and ways of looking at the world. And children from an early age like to retell stories they have heard. I remember a group of 3- and 4-year-olds patiently and very ably telling me the story of Goldilocks in their mother tongue because they thought I didn't know it.

Story pack

You might like to make a *story pack* which, once planned and prepared, can be used again and lent to other teachers.
Basically:

- Choose your story.
- Decide on the main things you hope the children will get out of it.
- Choose your activities to help the children to achieve these aims.
- Make or obtain the materials you will need: for example, a copy of the story, an authentic native-speaker book, pictures, word and sentence cards, tapes, material linked to the wider curriculum (for example, pictures of China, buffalos being used to plough the fields, etc. for 3.8, 'Ma Liang').

Reading corner

If you are lucky enough to have your own English room, then an important resource is the reading corner, a corner devoted to books and stories, including published books, books by the children, pictures, toys, and curious objects. Ideally it is a place where children can sit down and browse. There should be shelves with books, a table, a chair or two, a carpet, some cushions on the floor, and possibly a vase of flowers on the table. Each class should have at least two child librarians who check that the books are all properly signed in and out and that the corner is tidy and attractive.

Evaluation cards

Children can be asked to give their name and date of reading the book, and to classify it according to how interesting it is and how easy it is to read.

> Very interesting/interesting/not very interesting
> Very easy/easy/not very easy
> Comments

Borrowing chart

There can be a large chart on the wall in the corner on which the children identify the book and the date they are borrowing it.

Example

Book name	Name and date	Name and date	Name and date	Name and date
The Very Hungry Caterpillar	~~Karl 1.3.95~~			
Oh no, I'm a cat!	~~Alexander 3.6.95~~	Tomás 10.10.95		
Where's Spot?	~~Anne 2.3.95~~	Jules 8.7.95		
Sleeping Beauty	~~Tomás 4.4.95~~	Léa 7.6.95		

(Crossed out names mean a book has been returned.)
Alternatively, you can use a card index system.
The information needed is:

Name of child
Class
Title of book
Author of book
Date borrowed
Date returned
Librarian's signature.

Children can vote for their favourite books and put a 'Top Ten' on a wall poster to encourage reading. (This was suggested by María Pilar Estaún, who teaches in Molins de Rei, Spain.)

Activities before the story

Helping the children to understand the story

2.1 Choosing key new words

PREPARATION

Before the lesson:

1 Pick out the words which are essential to the story and which the children may not know.

2 Decide whether to teach them before the story (if they are easy to illustrate with a picture, mime, etc.) or during the story (if the story and the way you tell the story will help to give the meaning of the words).

2.2 Simplifying the language

LEVEL

Beginners

PREPARATION

Decide whether you want to simplify the language, but take into account the implications of losing the richness and rightness of the original. In some cases, if you change a word, you might change a meaning quite significantly and as a consequence have to change a lot of other words.

Less common vocabulary

over the stile → through the gate

Idioms

in a flash → quickly

Tenses

had been eating → ate

Word order

Into the sack jumped the little cat → The little cat jumped into the bag

Long sentences

The woodcutter, who had a kind heart, agreed → The kind woodcutter said, 'Yes'.

Introducing a new word

2.3 Pictures

Many objects, qualities, and action verbs can be illustrated by pictures. The pictures must obviously be big enough and clear enough to be seen and recognized from the back of the class.

PREPARATION

1 Prepare pictures which will help your children understand key words from the story.

The pictures can be:

- sketches by you or the children, on the board or on prepared picture flashcards
- illustrations in books
- magazine pictures.

2 Keep a 'picture bank' of illustrations which you find useful, filed by topic.

COMMENTS

For tips on how to draw or copy pictures quickly and easily, see Chapter 7, 'Pages to copy', and *1000 + Pictures for Teachers to Copy* by Andrew Wright (see Further Reading). For ways of using pictures, see *Pictures for Language Learning* by Andrew Wright (see Further Reading).

2.4 Objects

Objects (sometimes called 'realia') are an ideal way of showing the meaning of English words for concrete things.

IN CLASS

1 Show the children real objects connected with the story: for example, a drum and some fruit for 'Strange animal' (3.12).

2 Let the children touch, hold, and perhaps use them.

COMMENTS

This will appeal to those children who like tactile learning.

2.5 Mime

Many items of vocabulary, including actions, feelings of emotion, adjectives, and adverbs, can be communicated by mime.

IN CLASS   Use mime and actions to introduce new words before the story, and while you are telling it.

COMMENTS   Mime is particularly relevant to storytelling as it helps keep the children's attention and helps make the meaning much clearer.

2.6 Context

Some words are best understood in context, for example, a comparative form needs a comparison. Sometimes you can create contexts in the classroom in order to introduce a new word, but it may well be that the best context is the story itself.

2.7 Translation

IN CLASS   1 Sometimes translation is the fastest and most efficient way to say what a word means.

2 Once the children understand the meaning, concentrate on getting them to use the English word a lot and they will forget how they acquired it!

VARIATION   Tell the story partly in the learners' mother tongue and partly in English. Increase the amount of English each time you tell it. See 3.9, 'The prince and the dragon: lesson plan'.

Establishing a new word

Remember that understanding the meaning of a new word is not the same as learning it. It takes time and purposeful use to make a word one's own. Here are a few activities which might help the children to use the new word and slowly make it their own.

2.8 Memory game

IN CLASS   1 Show the children four to eight pictures or objects.

2 Then hide them and challenge the children to remember what they are and what they look like (in English).

VARIATION You might also remove one of the pictures and ask which one has been removed.

2.9 Picture–word matching

PREPARATION Prepare pairs of cards with pictures and the written form of the words you want the children to learn. If you have a photocopier, you can make several sets and the children can colour them in.

IN CLASS The children try to match the word card to the correct picture card. They should say the word out loud to practise the correct pronunciation.

2.10 Pelmanism

PREPARATION Prepare several pairs of cards: one with a picture and one with the English word on. Spread them out, face down.

IN CLASS In pairs or groups, the children take it in turns to try to remember what the cards are and which two go together.

1 A child points to the back of two cards saying, for example, '*witch* and *witch*'.

2 Then she or he turns the cards over. If one is the picture of a witch and the other is the word *witch*, then the child picks them up and keeps them.

3 If he or she is wrong then both cards must be turned upside down again but their position must remain the same. The winner is the child with most pairs of cards.

2.11 Bingo

There are many versions of this game but the easiest one is when you have introduced and practised about ten or twenty words.

PREPARATION Find or draw pictures of the words.

IN CLASS 1 Write ten to twenty words on the board.

2 Each child chooses any five words and writes them down. Make sure they do not all have the same words.

3 You call out one word after another and hold up a picture of it. Any child who has the word you call out can cross it off. When a child has crossed off all five words he or she shouts 'BINGO!'

VARIATIONS

This version of 'Bingo' only helps children to relate the spoken and written forms of words. In order to concentrate the children's minds on meaning, you can call out a definition of the word rather than the word itself, or hold up a picture, or mime the word.

2.12 Repeat it if it is true

IN CLASS

1 Show an object or a picture. Make a statement about it.

2 If the statement is true, the children should repeat it, and if it is not true they should remain silent.

2.13 Drawing

IN CLASS

1 Divide the children into teams of about eight.

2 Children from each team take it in turns to come to the board. As they come forward, give them a word. They try to illustrate the word so that their team can identify it.

3 If their team recognizes the word within one minute, they get a point.

2.14 Drawing and designing

IN CLASS

The children draw and design pictures and special letter shapes related to the new words.

COMMENTS

This can help some children to internalize the meaning of the words.

2.15 Personal picture dictionary

IN CLASS

The children make up their own picture dictionary for all the stories they hear with each story represented on one or two pages. Encourage the children to see how some key words occur in different stories.

VARIATION

An alternative design is for the children to arrange the words and pictures thematically in their books or folders.

2.16 Word webs

IN CLASS

The children invent their own 'word webs' of newly acquired and related words.

Word webs can be objective (showing connections shared by most people) or subjective (showing personal connections). See the example.

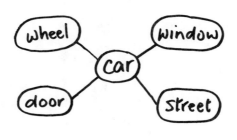

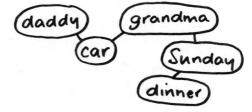

2.17 Mastermind

This game concentrates the children's minds mainly on the spelling of new words.

IN CLASS

1 Draw a short line on the board for each letter of the word you have chosen, for example, four lines for 'mice'.

2 Ask the children to think of English words with four letters. One child comes to the board and writes a four-letter word under the four lines.

3 If none of the letters in the child's word are the same as the letters in your word, write 'x' by it.

If any letters are the same as the target word but in the wrong positions, write 'o' for each correct letter.

If any letters are the same and in the correct positions, write a filled-in ● for each correct letter.

4 Different children try to guess the word and write their guess on the board. The child who guesses the correct word gets a point, and can choose the next word.

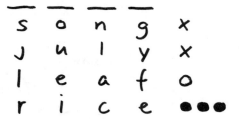

Acknowledgements
This example was supplied by Eva Benkö.

Helping the children to focus on the subject and to begin to predict what the story might be about

2.18 Front cover

If you are using a book, show the front cover (or just the title of the story) and ask the children to guess what it might be about.

2.19 Topics from pictures

IN CLASS

1 Show pictures from inside the book.

2 Ask the children to tell you as much as they can about the topic of the story. The topic or theme may be about anything: dragons, losing something, dangerous animals, painting pictures, wishing for something, China, and so on. For example, for 'Ma Liang' (3.8), show a map of China and some pictures of Chinese villages. Ask the children what they think, know, or have experienced about China.

FOLLOW-UP

This is a good introduction to topic work (see Chapter 4).

2.20 Guess the objects

PREPARATION

Wrap up objects related to the story, for example, a water-colour brush (preferably Chinese or Japanese) for the 'Ma Liang' story (3.8).

IN CLASS

1 Get the children to guess what it might be. Then tell them it will be in the story and that they can ask questions about it.

2 Let them find some things out about the story, then tell it to them.

2.21 Discuss

Discuss with the children anything they may know or feel about the topic of the story, relating it to their own experience. For example, before introducing 'The little duckling' (3.3), you might ask the children to tell you about all the birds and animals they know and which are the most beautiful parts of each one. Before introducing 'In a dark, dark town' (3.2), you might ask the children what is 'scary' (frightening) for them.

2.22 Give a story summary

You can give the children a summary of the story, perhaps in the mother tongue, before you tell it.

Help the children to predict the gist of the story and set them a task to do

2.23 Muddled pictures

LEVEL

Elementary and pre-intermediate

PREPARATION

Prepare a series of pictures of key moments in the story. You can photocopy and cut up the pictures for each pair of children, or display them on the board, each one with a letter.

IN CLASS

1 Show separate pictures from the story.

2 Ask the children to try to put them into the correct sequence. The children put the pictures or letters in the sequence they think the story will be in.

3 They then listen to the story to see if they were correct.

2.24 Children's pictures

IN CLASS

1 Give the children a brief description of what the story is about.

2 Ask each child or pair of children to draw a picture of a key moment or of a key character or place in the story. The pictures should be big enough to see when displayed on the board and should not show any background setting.

3 Put the pictures on the wall. Get the children to predict the story. Then tell it.

COMMENTS

This involves the children, helps them to predict the story, and makes them feel interested even before you begin.

2.25 Predicting

LEVEL

Pre-intermediate

IN CLASS

1 If the children know the story in their mother tongue, tell them you are going to tell it in English. Ask them to write down all the English words they think they will hear on separate pieces of paper.

2 When you tell the story they should put the pieces of paper into the order in which they hear them.

VARIATION

Give the children the first line or paragraph of the story and ask them to write down all the words they predict they will hear.

Example

From 'Little Red Riding Hood' (3.7):

mother daughter girl
red grandma wood
flower wolf house
bed eat

2.26 Children retelling

IN CLASS

1 If the story is well-known to the children in their own language, ask them to try to retell it.

2 You then tell the story in English and let them compare what they predicted with your version.

If the children are beginners they can retell the story in their mother tongue. If they are elementary or pre-intermediate, encourage them to use single words or short phrases in English if they cannot produce whole sentences every time.

Example

'Cinderella' is a well-known story within the European tradition and might be retold by elementary children like this:

There is a girl. She is poor. She is dirty. She is in a kitchen. She has two sisters. She goes to a dance. She has a beautiful dress. A man loves the girl. Midnight. She goes. Shoe. The shoe is small. It is her shoe. It is not her sisters' shoe. She marries the man.

2.27 Gapped story

LEVEL   Pre-intermediate

IN CLASS   1 Give the children a version of the story with gaps in the text.
You can put it on the board for classwork or on paper for
pairwork.

2 Ask them to read it and begin to imagine what words might be
missing. You can make the task easier by giving the children a
list of words to choose from.

3 Tell the story and they complete the gaps.

Example

The travellers and the bear

Two men were _ _ _ _ _ _ _ in a forest. Suddenly a bear
came. One man _ _ _ and climbed up a _ _ _ _. The
other _ _ _ couldn't _ _ _ and couldn't fight the _ _ _ _ by
himself so _ _ lay on the _ _ _ _ _ _. The _ _ _ _ came to
the _ _ _ and sniffed at his head. Then the _ _ _ _ went
away.
'What did the bear say?' said the _ _ _ in the _ _ _ _.

The _ _ _ on the ground _ _ _ _, 'The bear said, "Is he
your _ _ _ _ _ _ _? Why did _ _ leave _ _ _?"'

Words

friend said bear man ground man walking ran run he man tree
he bear tree he man bear man you

Photocopiable © Oxford University Press

COMMENTS   Gapped text activities are normally done *after* the story. More
techniques are given in 2.49, 'Gap filling' and 2.50, 'Information
gap filling'.

2.28 Ten key words

LEVEL   Pre-intermediate

IN CLASS   1 Write about ten key words or short phrases on the board in
the order in which they occur. Do not worry if a few of the
words are unknown to the children.

2 Ask them if they can predict the story (they can use the
present tense to do this).

3 Then tell the story.

VARIATION 1 You can ask higher-level learners to work in groups and to write down each word in a sentence which explains it.

VARIATION 2 Tell the class they can ask you three questions only—as a class.

Acknowledgements
Jim Wingate suggested Variation 2.

Activities during the story

You may decide that some of these activities can only be attempted during the *second* or *third* telling of the story.

Let the children listen to and enjoy the story

We must remember not to spoil the story in our eagerness to 'get a lot of useful work out of it'! Sometimes the best activity for the children is to sit and listen.

Helping the children to understand the story

It is easier for the children if you tell the story rather than read it (see page 14). The following techniques aid understanding:
- use pictures (drawn on the board by you or the children, pictures in the book, magazine pictures, flannelgraph figurines), objects, masks, and puppets
- use mime yourself or direct the children
- use sound effects
- mix mother tongue and English
- translate key words as you tell the story
- accept that some of the items of grammar can be learnt as vocabulary, for example, past tense forms.

Encourage the children to predict what is coming next

2.29 Stopping and asking

Stop whenever it seems appropriate and ask what the children think is going to happen next. At beginner level they can reply in their mother tongue, and at higher levels with short phrases or complete sentences in English.

Invite a personal response

2.30 Pictures in the mind

1 Every now and again, stop and ask the children to close their eyes and see if they can see a picture of the story in their mind. Ask them to share this picture with other children—theirs will be different.

2 You can also ask them what they can hear, feel, taste, and smell. Beginners can use their mother tongue and at higher levels they can use short phrases or complete sentences in English.

2.31 How would you feel?

Now and again, stop and ask the children how they would feel or what they would do in the situation in the story. At beginner level they can reply in their mother tongue, and at higher levels with short phrases or complete sentences in English.

2.32 What can you add?

At intervals, stop and ask the children for more information about things in the story. For example, you can ask what other sorts of food and drink Little Red Riding Hood might have in her basket (see 3.7). You can stop and ask what Ma Liang might draw in order to get away from the king and his soldiers (see 3.8). At beginner level learners can reply in their mother tongue, and at higher levels with short phrases or complete sentences in English.

Enable the children to show their understanding and to participate

2.33 Miming

The children mime an action, character, feeling, and so on from the story. They can mime at their desks or in a clear space in the classroom. For example, 'The little white cat' (3.6, page 92) can be mimed by each child using his or her fingers to represent the cat. 'The little Indian boy' (3.4) can be mimed by the children moving their bodies while sitting in their seats. And 'Little Red Riding Hood' (3.7) can be mimed by the children walking in a big circle, each one miming the part.

Example

1 The children listen to you telling (not reading) the story twice, each time miming with you.

2 They listen and mime a third time, but now you only tell the story and don't mime.

3 The fourth time you read the text of the story.

Acknowledgements
I adapted this idea from Jim Wingate.

2.34 Figurines

MATERIALS

Figurines on a magnet board or flannelboard or figures and scenes on an overhead projector, or even pictures blu-tacked to the board.

IN CLASS

The children can operate the figurines as you tell the story (or later when they retell the story themselves), which will show whether they understand.

2.35 Sequencing sentence cards or pictures

LEVEL

Elementary and pre-intermediate
If you gave the children sentence cards or pictures to put in order before the story (see 2.23, 'Muddled pictures'), they can now check them to see if they are in the correct sequence.

2.36 Jump up word card

IN CLASS

1 Give each child a word card before the story. You can either give each child a different word, or give the same word to several of them.

2 Ask them to jump up and sit down every time they hear their word.

VARIATION 1

1 Divide the class into As, Bs and Cs, and ask the Bs and Cs to look away from you while you show a card with two or three words on it to the As, and then the same for the other groups.

2 You then tell the story and the children jump up and sit down if they hear their word.

3 You can ask the children to notice what their neighbour's word is.

VARIATION 2

The children write down their favourite word and their least favourite word, and jump up every time they hear them. Their neighbour has to guess which two words they chose.

VARIATION 3

Ask them to jump up whenever they hear a certain kind of word, for example, a number, a colour, or an animal. But make sure this is more like a game than a test!

2.37 Displaying pictures

IN CLASS

If the children have drawn or been given pictures before the story (see 2.13, 'Drawing', 2.19, 'Topics from pictures', and 2.24, 'Children's pictures'), ask them to bring them to the front or hold them up at the appropriate moment in the story.

2.38 Expressive lines

LEVEL

Pre-intermediate
The children draw an expressive line showing how they feel about each stage in the story.

IN CLASS

1 Explain this idea before the story and say that you will stop every so often during the story for them to draw their line.

2 Afterwards they write a sentence under each line.

COMMENTS

For more on the use of expressive abstract lines see pages 36–8. Here is an example, taken from 'Strange animal' (3.12, page 123).

Ray began to pick fruit . Suddenly he turned..

2.39 Drawing and colouring

IN CLASS

The children draw and/or colour a person, an animal, or an object based on what they hear in the story. See the illustration below in which the teacher drew the original little duckling and the children added parts (see 3.3 'The little duckling', page 80).

2.40 Labelling a picture

This is suitable for the second or third telling.

PREPARATION

Draw a picture based on the story, or ask the children to draw one.

IN CLASS

1 Write key words from story on the board before the story begins.

2 As the children listen, ask them to write the words on a picture next to the relevant object or action.

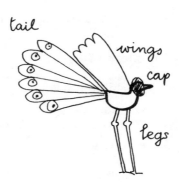

In this example the child made the drawing as he or she listened to the story of 'The little duckling' (3.3) and then, during the second telling, the child wrote the words next to the drawing.

The children can either draw or write on one big picture on the board, or each child does their own picture.

2.41 Using each sense

1 Tell the children the story and then repeat it.

2 The second time they must concentrate on all the things they can see.

3 The third time they concentrate on all the things they can hear, and so on.

4 Every so often you can stop and ask them to tell their neighbour or the whole class what they have experienced.

Examples

I saw a white cottage. The sun was shining.
I heard some birds and the wind.

In order for this activity to work well you must really tell the story with feeling!

Beginners can use their mother tongue, and elementary and pre-intermediate learners can say short phrases and sentences in English.

2.42 Phrases you like

Pre-intermediate

1 The children listen to the story several times.

2 They note down the words and phrases they like (and some they don't like) in the story.

3 They write a poem making use of them.

A simpler version of this activity is for the children just to repeat words they like, orally.

Participating orally

2.43 Chorusing

PREPARATION Select key sentences from the story which are suitable for speaking aloud.

IN CLASS The children repeat the key sentences after you, all together.

VARIATION The children make sound effects, for example, the wind, crazy voices, or knocking.

COMMENTS **1** This works especially well with stories which contain a lot of repetition. 'Ma Liang' (3.8) and 'The little duckling' (3.3) are both full of repeated sentences. Examples of verses for choral chanting for 'Ma Liang' are given on page 109.

2 Chorusing helps the children to learn and pronounce key vocabulary without making individual children speak in front of the whole class. See also the notes on choral reading in Chapter 1, page 22.

2.44 Chanting

Chanting is an extension of chorusing in which repetition is used together with rhythm and stress. The children chant in groups and other groups respond.

PREPARATION Select a few quite simple key lines from the story and practise speaking them in a rhythmic, chant-like form.

IN CLASS **1** The children repeat the lines after you.

2 Invite them to say other lines in this way once they have done a few directed by you. See 'The little white cat' (3.6) for some examples.

2.45 True or false?

LEVEL **Elementary and pre-intermediate**

IN CLASS **1** Tell a story the children know—perhaps a story they have just heard.

2 Make some changes and ask the children to put up their hands to tell you what you have said wrong.

Example

Little Red Riding Hood's father said, 'Take these sandwiches to your uncle'.

2.46 Whistling story

LEVEL

Pre-intermediate

IN CLASS

1 Tell a story with some words missing. Instead of saying the word you whistle (or make some other noise or gesture).

2 The children must tell you what the word is.

COMMENTS

You can make this easier for the children by writing the words on the board before you begin or by telling the story several times before you do the whistling story technique.

Activities after the story

Showing understanding through traditional exercises

There are numerous well-known, traditional exercises for showing understanding, for example: true/false questions, comprehension questions, and muddled sentences. We must remember that these exercises are rather different in spirit to the story and might spoil it for the children. Here I suggest some more interesting variations on these traditional techniques.

2.47 Children's comprehension questions

LEVEL

Pre-intermediate

IN CLASS

1 The children work in groups. Each group writes down five comprehension questions about the story.

2 Divide the class into new groups so that each child is the only one from his or her original group.

3 Each child then takes turns to ask the other children's questions.

VARIATION

The children write true/false questions for each other.

COMMENTS

They can only do this if they are familiar with comprehension questions and have some models to follow.

2.48 Muddled sentences or words

LEVEL

Elementary and pre-intermediate

PREPARATION

1 Choose key sentences from the story.

2 Either:
- write or type the sentences on to paper, make one photocopy for each child, and cut them up into single sentences;
- or write them on the board for the children to copy;
- or write the sentences on large strips of paper (one metre approximately) that the children can hold up.

IN CLASS

1 If necessary, the children copy the sentences on to sheets of paper and cut them up.

2 They try to arrange the sentences into the correct sequence, or copy them in the correct order into their books.

3 Once the children have made their sequence you can tell the story again and they can check if they have arranged their sentences correctly.

Example

Here is an example of muddled sentences from 'The little white cat' (3.6).

The witch said, 'Jump on my knee.'

'Goodbye, mum! I'm going to be a witch's cat!'

This little white cat has six brothers and sisters.

'Witches have black cats. Go away!'

There is a chimney sweep sitting behind the cottage.

'I can't see you because I am blind.'

VARIATION 1

The children can arrange key words instead of sentences in their proper sequence.

VARIATION 2	This activity can be done with pictures instead of words or sentences.
VARIATION 3	Instead of the children holding the word or sentence cards, they can clip them on to a clothes line which is tied across the room. This is an invaluable technique for sequencing words, sentences, and pictures.
COMMENTS	1 Some teachers use this activity before the children hear the story and thus use it as a prediction exercise and a way of whetting the children's appetite for the story. 2 This technique is very useful for early or even pre-readers because it relies on reading recognition of sentences they are familiar with orally. For pre-readers the use of pictures instead of words or texts allows them to show understanding without having to encounter the written text.

Showing understanding and retelling

2.49 Gap filling

LEVEL	**Elementary and pre-intermediate** There are a number of activities based on the idea of a gapped text.
PREPARATION	Prepare a text of the story, or part of it, on a photocopy or on the board, with gaps left where some words should be.
IN CLASS	1 Give out the text or write it on the board. 2 The class fill in the gaps, either with you or on their own.
COMMENTS	The number and type of words missing determine the difficulty of the task.
VARIATION 1	1 Give each child a photocopy of the text (or they can copy it from the board). 2 You dictate the full text. They fill in their gapped text.
VARIATION 2	1 Put a gapped text on the board. 2 The class call out the possible words and try to retell the story.
VARIATION 3	1 Put the text of the story on the board. 2 Erase certain words.

3 The children call them out and try to remember them.

4 You continue to erase words and they continue to try to remember what you have erased. In the end they are remembering the whole text.

VARIATION 4

1 Give the children, working in pairs, a complete text of a very short story they have heard and know well.

2 Ask them to rewrite the text and to leave out ten words in different places. They should write their text in pen.

3 They then exchange their gapped text with another pair and try to complete their neighbours' gapped text, using a pencil so that the text can be used again.

2.50 Information gap filling

You can combine gap filling with information gap activities to make the lesson more interesting.

LEVEL

Elementary and pre-intermediate

PREPARATION

Prepare two different versions of the same text, with gaps in different places.

IN CLASS

The children work in pairs. Each partner has the same text but with different gaps. They help each other to make a complete text.

VARIATION 1

In pairs, the children sit back to back. Child A can see a large, gapped text on the wall at one end of the room, and child B can see the same text but with different gaps at the other end of the room. They help each other to write out the complete text.

VARIATION 2

There are four large versions of the same text with different gaps, each displayed on a different wall. Each pair of children compiles a complete text by moving around the room from wall to wall.

2.51 Find the mistakes

LEVEL

Elementary and pre-intermediate

PREPARATION

You, or the children working in pairs, rewrite the story with mistakes of content in it (not grammar!).

IN CLASS   Other children must find the mistakes.

COMMENTS   It is easier if the children work from a copy of the correct text.

VARIATION   You or a child say one sentence with one change in it. Another child must say the sentence correctly. For example, 'Goldilocks ate all Daddy bear's porridge'—'No, Goldilocks ate all *Baby* bear's porridge!'

2.52 Describe and identify

LEVEL   **Elementary and pre-intermediate**

IN CLASS   1 Display a series of pictures from the story on the wall. (The children can draw these as a separate activity—see 2.24, 'Children's pictures'.)

2 You (or a child) describe or tell part of the story. Another child points at the relevant picture from the display. It can be done as a competition between two children to see who can be the first to identify the right picture.

2.53 Draw and guess

LEVEL   **Elementary and pre-intermediate**

IN CLASS   You (or a child) draw a picture from the story and the children guess which part of the story it illustrates.

VARIATION   1 The children listen to a story three times.

2 They draw one (or more) picture(s), then show it to their neighbour who should guess which part of the story the picture is from.

3 They listen to the story again and check their answers.

2.54 Da Di Da Da

LEVEL   **Pre-intermediate**

IN CLASS   You (or a child) imitate the rhythm and intonation of a key sentence in the story and see if the others can recognize which one it is.

COMMENTS

This only works if you and the children are very familiar with the story and if you choose rhythmically-outstanding sentences. But the children find it amusing if it is easy for them.

Example

What big ears you've got

Da da ^{di} da da

2.55 Retelling the story

LEVEL

Elementary and pre-intermediate

It is a perfectly reasonable activity to try to remember a story and to tell it to someone who has already heard it.

IN CLASS

The children try to retell the story, perhaps by moving pictures or by acting.

VARIATION

If retelling is done in pairs, the listener's job is to encourage and to help the teller get the story right.

2.56 Remove the pictures

LEVEL

Elementary and pre-intermediate

PREPARATION

Prepare a series of pictures which tell the story. The children can draw these in a previous activity (see 2.24, 'Children's pictures'), or you can use ones you prepared for activities before the story such as 2.13, 'Drawing', 2.23, 'Muddled pictures', 2.35, 'Sequencing sentence cards or pictures'.

IN CLASS

1 Display all the pictures. Go through the story again, eliciting as much of it as possible from the children, using the pictures as a memory aid.

2 The children then close their eyes and you remove one picture.

3 The children then open their eyes and tell you which picture is missing and which part of the story it represents.

4 The children close their eyes again. You now remove another picture and they tell you which one is missing.

5 Gradually remove all the pictures and see if they can retell the story from memory.

COMMENTS   You can make it easier for the children if you display sentence strips as captions to the pictures.

2.57 Jump on the pictures

LEVEL   Elementary and pre-intermediate

PREPARATION   Prepare a series of inexpensive pictures (photocopies or sketches) illustrating the story.

IN CLASS   1 Stand the children in a circle. Put the pictures in the circle.

2 The children take it in turns to jump on to a picture and to say two or three words, short phrases, or full sentences about it.

2.58 Stepping stone pictures

LEVEL   Elementary and pre-intermediate

PREPARATION   Prepare a series of inexpensive pictures (photocopies or sketches) illustrating the story.

IN CLASS   1 Arrange the pictures on the floor in a line.

2 Challenge the learners to walk from picture to picture telling the story. If you say there are sharks in the river they will find it a double challenge to remember the story!

VARIATION   If you have access to a floor made of large tiles then you can do the following activity. The children can go from one tile to another if they can add a sentence to the retelling of the story. Their aim is to cross the floor.

COMMENTS   This activity is suitable for small classes or for groups working by themselves.

2.59 Story flowchart

IN CLASS   1 Show the children how to make a flowchart of the story they have been listening to.

2 In pairs or groups, the children make their own.

Here is a story flowchart for 'Elidor' (3.13, page 129).

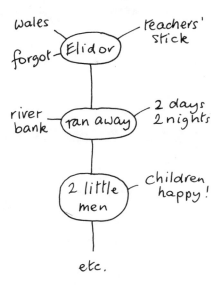

COMMENTS   Flowcharts help the children to become conscious of the way a story is structured. They also help the children to retell the story.

2.60 Story analysis

LEVEL   Pre-intermediate

IN CLASS   1 Help the children to analyse the story into settings, characters, problems, events, and resolution.

2 The children can then experiment by changing the elements one by one and changing the story.

These analytical elements can be shown in the bubbles of a flowchart (see the activity above). They can also be summarized and clipped to a clothes line across the room. The children can then rearrange the story elements by literally changing the order on the clothes line.

2.61 Drawing a map

IN CLASS   The children draw a map of the story and mark off a route, numbering the key points.

COMMENTS

Stories relevant for this include 'Little Red Riding Hood' (3.7), 'The little Indian boy' (3.4), and 'Elidor' (3.13). The activity is described in more detail using 'Elidor' as an example on page 133.

2.62 Throw the ball and continue the story

LEVEL

Pre-intermediate

IN CLASS

A child begins the story and then throws a paper ball to another child who must continue it.

COMMENTS

This is a challenging activity and only for children who you feel know the story very well and have enough English.

2.63 Pass the picture and tell the story

LEVEL

Elementary and pre-intermediate

IN CLASS

1 Stand in a circle with the children.

2 Hold up a picture and briefly tell the part of the story which goes with it.

3 Give the picture to the child on your left, who must repeat the sentence(s) you said.

4 That child then passes it to her or his neighbour, who does the same thing.

5 When the class is confident, you can have several pictures moving at the same time.

COMMENTS

The children may not understand all the words they say because they are just copying you; however, this is a first step in articulating a phrase or sentence of the story and a safe opportunity to begin to associate meanings by holding the picture. When there are several pictures moving, then, clearly, the children must have a more discriminating grasp of the appropriate thing to say.

2.64 Whispering story

LEVEL Pre-intermediate

PREPARATION Write out about ten sentences from a short story. Make two more copies and cut these into strips.

IN CLASS

1 Display the sentences, in the correct sequence, on a table at the back of the classroom.

2 Place copies of all the sentences on separate strips of paper, out of order, on two desks near the front of the classroom. The desks should be about two metres apart.

3 Divide the class into two teams. Line them up behind the two desks.

4 One child from each team goes to the story text at the back of the classroom, reads the first line, and then runs to the first child in his or her team and whispers the sentence to him or her, who must whisper it to the child in front, and so on down the line.

5 The last child goes to the desk, picks up the correct sentence, and displays it on the board.

6 This child now runs to the story text at the back of the class and whispers another sentence to his or her team.

7 The first team to finish correctly is the winner.

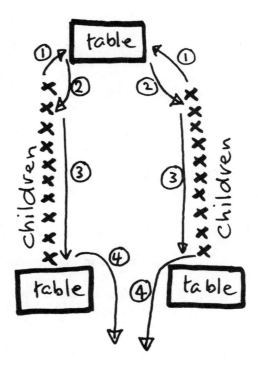

2.65 Growing story

LEVEL

Pre-intermediate

IN CLASS

1 Divide the class into two teams and ask them to stand in two rows at the back of the class. Divide the board into two parts.

2 The first child in each group runs to the board and writes the first word of the story and then runs back again to the back of his or her team. The second child then runs to the front and adds the second word of the sentence, and so on.

The aim is to see how much each team can write correctly in three minutes. The children can help each other and prepare the child who is next in turn to write on the board.

The sentences do not need to be exactly as they are in the story, but must be correct to get full marks!

2.66 Mixing two stories

LEVEL

Elementary and pre-intermediate

PREPARATION

Write out sentences from two stories on strips of paper and mix them up. Make a copy for each group.

IN CLASS

1 Put the children into groups.

2 Elementary level: ask the children to sort the sentences into two groups, one for each story.

Pre-intermediate level: ask the children to sort the sentences into two groups and then to sequence them properly.

VARIATION

You can ask the children to do the preparation: they mix up sentences from two stories and give them to other groups to sort out.

2.67 Likes and dislikes diagram

LEVEL

Elementary and pre-intermediate

IN CLASS

The children draw a diagram to show which character in the story likes/doesn't like which other, or who knows or doesn't know whom.

Example

This diagram shows relationships between characters in 'The little white cat' (3.6).

2.68 Words for characters

LEVEL

Elementary and pre-intermediate

IN CLASS

1 Give examples of words or short phrases which are, in your opinion, appropriate as a description of one of the characters in the story. For example, in 'Strange animal' (3.12), one might choose characteristics as follows:

Auntie: not kind, not generous, unhappy, stupid.

Father and mother: kind, generous, brave, good.

Strange animal: bad, nasty, evil, unhappy.

2 You might begin by brainstorming all the words and phrases on the board that the children can say about people: good, bad, happy, unhappy, nice, nasty, evil, generous, kind, intelligent, stupid, brave, and so on.

3 Ask the children to say which word or words fit each character most appropriately. Be open to the children interpreting the characters quite differently from you! There cannot be a right or a wrong answer!

2.69 Picture of a character

LEVEL   **Elementary**

IN CLASS   1 The children choose a character from the story and draw a picture of what they think their character looks like.

2 They write on one side of the paper what he or she likes and on the other side what he or she doesn't like. The writing can be done on a fold of paper which can then be turned over so that both texts can be seen next to the picture.

Example from 'Ma Liang' (3.8):

Helping children to show understanding and express themselves

2.70 Evaluating the story

IN CLASS   1 Ask the children to tell you what they thought of the story. Tell them you would like to know whether to use the story again with another class. You can use their mother tongue with beginners and elementary learners, and English with pre-intermediate children.

Here are some questions you can ask them:

Did you enjoy the story?	very much/a bit/not very much/not at all.
Did you understand the story?	most of it/a bit of it/not much of it/nothing.
Which was the best part?	when . . .
Which was the worst part?	when . . .
Which was a funny part?	when . . .
Which was an exciting part?	when . . .

VARIATION 1	The children can draw happy or sad faces to show how much they liked the story.

| VARIATION 2 | Beginners and elementary-level children can express their approval or lack of it by whispering 'a little' or shouting 'a lot' in answer to your question *How much did you like the story?* |

| VARIATION 3 | They can show the part of the story they liked best by standing next to the picture which illustrates it (if you have displayed them). |

| COMMENTS | For more ideas on feedback from the children, see *Young Learners* by Sarah Phillips in this series. |

2.71 Acting out

The children act out the story as you retell it.

IN CLASS

1 Divide the story, with the children's help, into different scenes.

2 Discuss what you will need and allocate roles. Objects in the classroom or the children themselves can represent objects in the story: for example, a cupboard can represent a mountain, and children can represent trees, doors, or anything. This planning phase is a way of checking their understanding of the story.

3 Some of the children act the story as you retell it.

COMMENTS

See also 2.94, 'Guidelines for dramatizing stories' (page 70).

2.72 Make a video or sound recording

IN CLASS

1 The children divide the story into scenes, with the location and the characters listed for each one. They may need help with this.

2 If you do it as a class then you can divide the class into groups, one group for each scene. Each group is then responsible for its scene.

3 They practise their scene and then perform it for the rest of the class. The other children must guess which scene they performed. They use whatever English they can cope with.

4 When they are confident, record the scenes in order.

2.73 Mime and guess

LEVEL   **Elementary and pre-intermediate**

PREPARATION   Write out ten sentences from the story which can be mimed.

IN CLASS   1 In groups, the children choose a sentence and take turns to mime it.

2 The others try to guess the sentence they are miming.

VARIATION   **For beginners:**

Tell each group their sentence privately, so that the others don't hear.

COMMENTS   Either all the children take on the same character and all mime the same actions at the same time, or each child represents a different character in a scene. Some children can take the parts of inanimate objects, for example, trees, doors, and so on.

2.74 Three key moments

LEVEL   **Pre-intermediate**

IN CLASS   1 The children choose and write down three sentences describing three key moments from the story.

2 They compare these with their neighbour's choice, and then with another two neighbours.

VARIATION   You might like to approach this activity by first of all collecting from the class a whole range of favourite moments and writing them on the board. The children then select the ones which are true for them.

Help the children to show their understanding and to create something

Here are some ideas which move from passive comprehension to involving the children's own ideas. For more on story-making, see the companion book to this one, *Creating Stories with Children* by Andrew Wright, in this series.

2.75 Retelling with opposites

LEVEL Pre-intermediate

IN CLASS The children retell the story but give the opposite of each noun, adjective, etc. For example, it is not a little white cat but a big black dog. If they cannot think of an opposite then they should change the word to something very different.

2.76 Adding information

LEVEL Elementary and pre-intermediate

IN CLASS Through discussion, you and the class can build up an enormous amount of detailed information about the characters and the setting in the story (depending on the language the children have). For example, for 'The little white cat' (3.6), you and the children can describe in detail: the witch's cottage, the little white cat's daily life with her witch, the recipe of magic to cure the witch's blindness, a telephone call from the little white cat to her mother, a letter from the little white cat to her family. It is not essential for the children to use full sentences.

Here are some examples:

Witch's cottage

small; two windows and a door; two little rooms, a kitchen and a bedroom; a fire; a cupboard; her brush (broomstick) is in the cupboard; her sweets are in the cupboard; her witch's cookbook is in the kitchen; her fridge is in the kitchen; she has got frogs in it.

The little white cat's day

At 7 a.m. my witch wakes up. At 8 a.m. I wake up. My witch makes tea. I drink my tea. At 8.30 a.m. I get up. At 8.45 a.m. I wash my face . . .

Magic recipe

One green frog, two purple flowers, three old hats, four red apples, five blue cats . . .

The little white cat's letter

Dear Mum, I have got a job. I am a witch's cat. Love from Little White Cat.

2.77 Drawing pictures

IN CLASS

1 The children draw two pictures from the story, one of a scene they like and one of a scene they don't like.

2 They write one or two sentences under each one.

COMMENTS

Beginners can just draw pictures of their favourite scene.

Little Red Riding Hood sees a wolf. The wolf says, Hello!

2.78 Making a book

The children write and illustrate a book of the story as a class or in groups, in pairs, or as individuals.

IN CLASS

1 If the children are working in groups, make each child responsible for one page. The group decides together what will be on each page and makes sure that the pages follow on from each other.

2 Give beginners sentences to copy and illustrate. Elementary and pre-intermediate learners can draft their sentences, show them to you, and then write them neatly on to the page they are responsible for (if they are working in groups).

COMMENTS

An easy way of making books is given on page 174. For more on making books, see *Creating Stories with Children* in this series.

2.79 Design a book cover

IN CLASS

The children design a book cover for the story, including an illustration and the title. Their choice of letter design and their illustration may reflect what they understand and feel about the story.

2.80 Writing letters

LEVEL

Elementary and pre-intermediate

IN CLASS

Ask the children to write letters from one character to another in the story. This can be part of a wider topic on learning how to write letters.

2.81 Writing a journal

LEVEL

Elementary and pre-intermediate

IN CLASS

The children write a journal of a typical day in the life of one of the characters, for example, the wolf in 'Little Red Riding Hood' (3.7).

2.82 Writing and performing a dialogue

LEVEL

Elementary and pre-intermediate

IN CLASS

1 Divide the children into groups. Give each group a separate scene from the story to work on.

2 The children write and perform a dialogue between two inanimate objects in the story, for example, the cottage door and the basket in 'Little Red Riding Hood'.

VARIATION   The children perform a dialogue which you have prepared for them, perhaps one which practises a certain language point.

COMMENTS   For more guidance see 2.94, 'Guidelines for dramatizing stories', page 70.

2.83 Continuing the story

LEVEL   **Pre-intermediate**

IN CLASS   The children invent a continuation of the story, in writing or orally.

Example

'Strange animal' (3.12) might be continued like this:
Ray went to the cliffs every day. There was a lot of fruit. Nobody went to the cliffs. They were frightened of the strange animal. Ray played his drum. His music was great. The strange animal liked Ray. One day Ray gave the strange animal a drum. The strange animal played new rhythms. Ray learnt the new rhythms and became a famous drummer.

2.84 Inventing a story from within the story

LEVEL   **Pre-intermediate**

IN CLASS   The children invent a story or a poem (it doesn't have to rhyme!) which arises out of one of the incidents in the story and explains it.

Example

Here is a poem about Elidor as he hides by the river bank (see 3.13, page 129).

> Where's Elidor?
> Where's Elidor?
> Elidor is by the river.
> He is hiding.
> Where's Elidor?
> Where's Elidor?
> Elidor is angry and sad.

He is thinking.
Where's Elidor?
Where's Elidor?
All the teachers said.

2.85 Making music

IN CLASS

The children make music to illustrate the mood or events in the story. The music can be instrumental or, more simply, percussion (including rhythmic tapping and humming).

Examples

For 'In a dark, dark town' (3.2), the children can slap their thighs in time to the rhythm of the story.

In 'Strange animal' (3.12), the children can create their own drums using their desks or the floor. (I once had one hundred and fifty 8- to 10-year-olds slapping the floor during my telling of 'Strange animal'!)

VARIATION

You can control the volume and the speed of the children's rhythmic tapping and humming by showing them flash cards:

Slowly	Quickly	Softly	Loudly

2.86 Geometrical shapes

LEVEL

Pre-intermediate

PREPARATION

Prepare a set of geometrical shapes: circles, squares, triangles, etc. You can cut them out of card but you can also buy them from educational suppliers.

IN CLASS

1 Divide the children into groups of about five. Give each group a set of shapes.

2 Tell the children they must work out how to tell the story and illustrate it with the shapes.

3 Groups then tell their stories for each other.

COMMENTS

Experience shows that children soon become imaginative with these geometrical shapes.

2.87 Interviewing a protagonist

LEVEL

Pre-intermediate

IN CLASS

1 You (or a child) take on the role of one of the protagonists (or antagonists) from the story and sit in front of the class.

2 You might begin this activity by asking the children to write down ten questions they would like to ask the character.

3 The class ask any questions they want to.

Example

You are the wolf in 'Little Red Riding Hood' (3.7):

Why did you eat Little Red Riding Hood?
Why don't you eat bread and cheese?
What music do you like?
What's your favourite colour?

VARIATION

1 Divide the class into groups. Each group represents one protagonist from the story.

2 Each group tries to answer the same five questions, for example:

Who am I?
What did I do?
How did I feel?
Who did I meet?
What was she or he like?

3 Then pair off children from different groups and let them ask and answer the questions.

2.88 Your own experience

IN CLASS

1 Ask the children to think about what happens in the story. Has anything similar happened to them?

2 The children talk about their experiences, in their mother tongue if they are beginners or elementary, and with single words and short phrases in English if they are pre-intermediate level.

2.89 Retell the story

IN CLASS

The children retell the story from a particular character's point of view or set the story in a different time.

Encourage them by eliciting ideas and words.

Beginners can use their mother tongue, perhaps supported and guided by your questions. Elementary and pre-intermediate learners can attempt to retell the story with single words and short phrases in English.

VARIATION   Pre-intermediate children can rewrite the story for a different medium, for example, for sound or for video recording.

2.90 Chapter titles

LEVEL   **Pre-intermediate**

IN CLASS   1 Divide the story into sections (chapters) with the children— this is possible even with very short stories.

2 The children work in groups and give each section a title.

3 The class then decide which is the best title for each section.

VARIATION   You might give the children a list of possible titles and ask them to put them into their preferred order.

2.91 Story scrabble

LEVEL   **Pre-intermediate**

IN CLASS   1 Write a sentence from the story on the board. The children write it in their books or on sheets of paper.

2 The children write words from the story vertically, including one letter from the sentence you have written.

Example

Here is an example from 'The little white cat' (3.6) done by a teacher and her class of elementary ten- and eleven-year-olds familiar with the story:

```
             H                          D
    SHB    SA      S   B         T      O
    THERE IS A LITTLE WHITE C AT
    ERO    X    N   SHOA        AS  S   R
      T         D   TIOC            T   N    E
      WHITE         EN KNOW         T
      E             RK
    PARENTS         SS
      S
```

3 Then ask the children to write as many sentences as they can with the words they have created. The sentences should tell the story.

Example

Here is a little white cat. She has six brothers and sisters. Her parents and her brothers are black. She doesn't know that she is white. She thinks she is black too.

VARIATION

To make this easier for the children, you could give all the words needed in jumbled order.

2.92 Reading race

LEVEL

Elementary and pre-intermediate

IN CLASS

1 Put the children into pairs.

2 Give each pair a copy of either a very short story or a selection of about fifteen lines from a longer story.

3 The children take it in turns to read the sentences—they can read one or two each time. The aim is to be the one who reads the last sentence.

2.93 Favourite characters

The children talk about fictional characters, and compose and act out dialogues.

LEVEL

Elementary

MATERIALS

Art materials for drawing.

PREPARATION

Ask the children to bring from home pictures of their favourite story characters (from books, comics, videos, television programmes, and so on).

IN CLASS

1 With the children in a semicircle around you, ask each child who brought something to stand with you and show the picture of their favourite character to the class.

2 Talk about the characters. Look for opportunities to use sentence structures the children know, like the ones in the examples below, and to summarize the story or to say the sort of things the character does.

Examples

Who's this?
It's (Robin Hood).
This is (Cinderella).
That's (Goldilocks).
Where's Baby Bear?
There he is.
What is she/he called in English?
I don't know.
In English she/he's called (Sleeping Beauty).
He's/she's a (king, prince, princess, poor girl, poor boy, hero, heroine).
He/she has got (a cat, a castle, a lot of money, a bow and arrow) (hasn't got any money).
He/she has got (long hair, golden hair, a long nose).
He/she can (fly through the air, make magic).
He/she is (funny, sweet, nasty, fantastic, frightening, horrible).
He/she lives in a (forest/house/cave).
She flies through the air.
He/she eats the little bear's porridge.

3 Ask the child with you to repeat one or two key phrases until he or she can do it well. Then ask the class to repeat the same phrases together.

4 Write these on the board (if you have introduced the written word).

5 Let each child show her or his pictures. Try to use the same sentence patterns about each character. If you are using the written word then you might build up lists of sentences of a similar kind.

6 If a lot of children have brought in books then this may get too much! So ask them to draw one or two characters once you have taken four children's pictures and to write the key phrases or key words with each one.

7 Make an exhibition of the books, videos, etc. which have been brought.

8 Ask children who have finished their own drawings to write labels for you about the books, videos, etc. The labels should contain at least three sentences and be placed next to the picture they are referring to.

9 Game
You or a child describe one of the characters and the other children guess who you have described.

You or a child: *She's got golden hair and she eats the little bear's porridge.*

Children: *Goldilocks!*

Once the characters are established they can be used in a variety of ways.

FOLLOW-UP 1

You can invent new stories about them, for example, 'Goldilocks and Robin Hood'. This provides a wonderful opportunity to give the female characters a new personality—strong, intelligent, brave, etc. instead of just beautiful!

FOLLOW-UP 2

The characters can become a living community whenever you want to give examples of language use. For example, a lot of the characters go on a picnic together. What sort of food do they take?

FOLLOW-UP 3

The children can dress up as a fictional character or draw their character on a piece of paper and hold it in front of themselves. The children then move around the class. They guess one another's characters:

> Child 1: *Do you live in a forest?*
> Child 2: *Yes.*
> Child 3: *Are you Robin Hood?*
> Child 2: *Yes.*

2.94 Guidelines for dramatizing stories

Depending on the age and experience of your children, you can either do the preparations yourself beforehand, or with the children in class.

1 Divide the story into sections which, if possible:

- are in the same setting
- have more or less the same characters
- take more or less the same time to act
- can be turned into a dialogue plus a monologue spoken by a narrator
- can be learnt, practised, and performed easily.

2 Consider having a narrator who:

- introduces the scene
- introduces the characters
- introduces the props and says what they are supposed to be
- reads the narration.

3 Consider having a chorus which:

- echoes the narrator's lines
- echoes the character's lines.

4 Divide up the inanimate object roles:

- children can be trees, gates, houses, beds
- the children playing inanimate objects could act as a chorus

– the children playing inanimate objects can make observations on what is happening.

5 Actors and inanimate objects must:

– speak their lines clearly to the 'audience' and aim for their voice to be clear enough to be heard at the back of the classroom
– speak slowly and with a variety of voices and feelings
– make lively appropriate gestures
– try not to stand with their backs to the 'audience'
– be easily identifiable from one scene to the next—i.e. the same character in the following scene must wear the same key feature, for example, a hat or coat, or carry the same bag.

Consider having masks and using make-up.

6 Decide on a maximum performance time and keep to it.

7 Use furniture and aisles, etc. as imaginary places: 'This cupboard is a mountain.'

8 Design and make posters and a programme (including a synopsis, advertising, and so on).

9 Have an interval with real drinks and music, with price and name labels for food (for example, *Biscuits 5 pence each*). There could be a programme for sale written in English. You could also agree with the children things they might say in the interval, for example:

Can I have an orange drink, please? I like . . . best. He/she's very funny.

Topic work

Stories can often be related to topics and a wide variety of activities. For examples, see Chapter 4, 'Topics and stories' (page 149).

3 Stories and lesson plans

In this section there are fifteen stories grouped according to the language level required to do the activities in the accompanying lesson plans. Each story is followed by ideas for activities. The activities are adapted from Chapter 2, 'A store of 94 activities', and demonstrate how these can be put together to make one lesson or several lessons. Most of the lesson plans given here average 40 minutes. However, each of your classes is different and each needs a lesson which is planned with their needs in mind. You will want to adapt the plans given here to your own circumstances. For example, I have not included warm-up activities to adjust the children's minds to the lesson, as these are partly dependent on what the previous lesson was or whether they have just come in from a lunch break or arrived at school after a rainstorm.

Guidelines for lesson planning

- Decide what your aim or aims are in deciding to use a story as the focus of your lesson: structural, functional, lexical, phonological, skills? Is it enough for the children to listen or to repeat, or do you want them to experiment and try to make use of all the language at their command?
- Decide how you can help the children to focus their minds on the content of the story and on the activities you want them to do.
- Decide which are the key language items they must understand or which they must use productively.
- Consider the whole lesson as an experience for the children. Is there enough variety of ways of learning: music, movement, drawing, and so on? Is there enough variety of pace: slow, quiet activities and brisk, noisy ones? Is there a good balance between active and receptive activities?

Beginners

3.1 Mr Page's pet shop

Story	Instructions
This is Mr Page's pet shop.	*Indicate the classroom.*
What's in the pet shop? Oh, there are some cats in the pet shop. Where are the cats?	*Take a picture word card.* *Give out several pictures of cats.*
What does a cat say? It says, 'Miaow! Miaow!'	
What's in the pet shop? Oh, there are some frogs in the pet shop. Where are the frogs?	*Take a picture word card.* *Give out several pictures of frogs.*
What does the frog say? It says, 'Croak! Croak!'	*Introduce more picture word cards until each child has an animal:* Dog: 'Woof! Woof!' Snake: 'Hiss! Hiss!' Parrot: 'Hello! Hello!' Mouse: 'Squeak! Squeak!' Turtle: 'Crunch! Crunch!' Rabbit: 'Nibble! Nibble!' Fish: 'Bubble! Bubble!' Pig: 'Grunt! Grunt!'
Now all the animals and the birds and the fish are talking. What a noise! Quiet please! Quiet please!	*General noise of all the children making their noises.* *Use a volume card to slowly raise the noise and then slowly diminish it.*
Now, here's a sausage. The dogs like it. They say, 'Yum! Yum!' And Piggy likes it and he says 'Yum! Yum!' The fish don't like it. They say, 'Yuk! Yuk!'	*Show the word and picture cards of food to the children. If they like it they should say, 'Yum! Yum!'* *If they don't like it they should say, 'Yuk! Yuk!'* *They should all do this at the same time. Control the noise with the volume card.*
Here's a worm! The fish and the snake and Piggy like it.	

They say, 'Yum! Yum!'
The dog, the cat, the parrot,
the rabbit, and the turtle don't
like it.
They say, 'Yuk, Yuk!'

Here's some chocolate!
Who likes chocolate?

Most of the creatures say, 'Yum! Yum!' But the fish, for example, may say, 'Yuk! Yuk!'
Go through all the food cards in this way and let the children make whatever noise they like. Control the volume of the noise with your volume cards! Make sure that Piggy says, 'Yum, Yum!' to all the foods.

But today is Piggy's birthday.
Piggy, invite the pets to your
birthday party!

The child playing the part of Piggy must now call out the name of each animal. Each animal responds with its noise.

And, of course, all the pets
sing a Happy Birthday song for
Piggy!

The children sing 'Happy Birthday' using their animal noises.

Now Piggy says,
'Help yourselves!
There's cheese!'

Piggy repeats, 'Help yourselves, There's cheese!' etc.
Piggy picks up each of the food cards and reads out the different foods. As he does so each animal, all at the same time, either says, 'Yum! Yum!' or 'Yuk! Yuk!'

Here comes Mr Page.
He's walking up the stairs.
One, two, three . . .
Piggy says, 'Quick! Go back to
your cages!'
Then Piggy eats up all the
food.

Walk round and round as if on a spiral staircase.

Piggy repeats 'Quick! Go back to your cages!'
Piggy picks up all of the food cards from the table and pretends to eat them.

Mr Page says, 'Good night,
animals! Sleep well!'
And all the pets are quiet
except Piggy who says, 'Yum!
Yum!'

Piggy says, 'Yum! Yum!'

Mr Page's pet shop: lesson plan

In this lesson plan the children only have to recognize the pictures they are shown in order to make the right noise. But they experience living in a story in which every child takes part.

LEVEL	**Beginners**
AGE	**6 to 9**
TIME	**30 minutes**
LANGUAGE	**Listening and slowly becoming familiar with a range of vocabulary for animals and food**

PREPARATION

1 Learn the story (see the tips on page 15).

2 Prepare picture word cards for animals and for food. The cards should be about 15 cm × 8 cm. The picture should be on one side and the word on the other.
Several children can be the same animal so you do not need to have a different animal for every child, nor for every item of food.
Each child should have an animal card.
Here are some suggestions:

Animals

cat dog fish parrot frog turtle rabbit mouse snake crocodile pig

Food

chocolate biscuit cheese insect worm sausage meat cabbage fruit leaves grass

For how to draw animals, etc., see section 7, page 209.

3 Prepare volume cards: about 15 cm × 8 cm.

On	Off	Loudly	Softly

IN CLASS

1 Tell the children (in their mother tongue if necessary) that you are going to tell them a story about a pet shop and that they are going to be the creatures in the shop.

2 Ask what animals they think might be in the pet shop.

3 Hold out a spread of animal cards for a few children to choose one each. Tell the class what each child has chosen and show the picture and the word for it. Make sure that the child practises the noise the creature makes. (Remember that animal noises can be different in different languages!)

4 Do this until everyone has a card. Of course, you can get everyone to practise the noises that all the creatures make. Finally, ask all the children to each make their own noise.

You might like to explain that the representation of animal noises is different in most languages. In English there are the following conventions: cats (miaow); dogs (woof woof or bow bow); pigs (grunt grunt or a noise like staccato snoring.) The other animals' noises are open to individual interpretation. Control the volume with your volume cards. Finally, make them silent with the 'Off' card.

5 Then begin to pick up the food cards, one by one. Tell the children to say, 'Yum! Yum!' if they think their animal likes the food, and 'Yuk! Yuk!' if they think their animal does not like the food. Stress that Piggy likes all the food and says 'Yum! Yum!' every time.

6 Finally, tell the children it is Piggy's birthday and he (or she) invites all the animals to his (or her) party. Piggy should stand up in a clear space and call out each animal's name and each animal should make its noise as it is called and stand up and join Piggy.

7 All the animals should now sing 'Happy Birthday' in their animal language to Piggy.

8 Piggy then picks up a food card says, 'Help yourselves! There's cheese!' etc. Each animal says 'Yum! Yum!' or 'Yuk! Yuk!' as appropriate for each of the foods which Piggy names.

9 Now you, the teacher, can imitate the footsteps of Mr Page the pet shop owner coming up the stairs. Piggy says, 'Quick! Go back to your cages!'

10 Piggy then 'eats up' all the food (picking up the food cards), and Mr Page comes in and says, 'Good night, animals! Sleep well!'.

FOLLOW-UP 1

The children might like to draw their creature and make a list of what it likes to eat and what it doesn't like to eat. They should write down anything they wish, checking it with you.

My fish likes: insects, sandwiches, and ice-cream. Yum! Yum!
My fish doesn't like: mice, sausages, and apples. Yuk! Yuk!

FOLLOW-UP 2

If you want the children to remember most of the vocabulary then they must make more extensive use of the new words they have met in the story. They could write:

Danny's parrot likes mice, sausages, seeds, and cake. Yum! Yum!
Danny's parrot doesn't like soup, ice-cream, and oranges. Yuk! Yuk!

3.2 In a dark, dark town

In a dark, dark town
There is a dark, dark road.

And in the dark, dark, road
There is a dark, dark house.

And in the dark, dark house
There is a dark, dark door.

Go in the door.

There are some dark, dark stairs.

Go up and up and up and up
And up and up and up
The dark, dark stairs.

Now . . .

There is a dark, dark room.

Go in the dark, dark room.

In the dark, dark room
There is a dark, dark cupboard.

Open the dark, dark cupboard.

What is there?

In a dark, dark town: lesson plan

This highly adaptable story can be simply listened to and acted out, or can be learnt by heart, or can lead to highly imaginative additions.

LEVEL	**Beginners and above, depending on the activity you choose**
AGE	**6 to 12**
TIME	**30 minutes**
LANGUAGE	*There is*; adjectives and nouns
PREPARATION	1 Learn the story by heart. 2 Make a cupboard. Use a large piece of paper, folded, with a cupboard door drawn on one side. Or better still, cut the bottoms out of two large, flat cardboard boxes and hinge them together. Draw panels of a cupboard door on one, including a handle.
IN CLASS	1 Show the illustrations to the story on the overhead projector or give each pair of children a copy. Ask the children how many words they can give you about the pictures. Help them to include: *town, road, house, door, stairs, room, cupboard*. Teach the word *dark* by saying that each object is dark. If there is any doubt put your head in the cupboard in your room or cover your eyes.

2 Tell the story several times until the children can repeat it with you.

3 Let them mime it at their desks with books for buildings and a ruler for a road and an imaginary door to open. The children can move their fingers for walking up the stairs.

4 Ask the children to imagine with you different things which could be in the cupboard. Ask for a noun and an adjective if you would like them to practise adjectives. Write the ideas on the board. Encourage the children to ask for words they don't know. Teach them the question *What's (mother tongue word) in English?*. Use your dictionary if you don't know the word a child asks for.

Examples

There is an old elephant in the cupboard.
There are ten cows in the cupboard.
There is an angry teacher in the cupboard.

5 Ask every child to draw one of the ideas and then to stick them inside the cupboard you have made.

6 Put the children in pairs and ask them to compile their ten favourite phrases and to write them decoratively in their books complete with one or two illustrations.

7 Ask every child to draw small versions of some of the things they thought of and to stick them inside the cupboard you have made. As they stick them inside, see how many of the objects which are already inside the cupboard they can name (complete with their adjectives).

Acknowledgements
I first heard this story told in this way by the great West Indian storyteller, Grace Hallworth. In the original version, in the cupboard there is an electrician mending the fuse!

3.3 The little duckling

The little duckling sees a peacock.
'What a beautiful tail! I want a beautiful tail, too!'
Suddenly the little duckling has a big, beautiful peacock's tail!
The little duckling is very pleased.

The little duckling sees a flamingo.
'What beautiful legs! I want beautiful legs, too!'
Suddenly the little duckling has long, thin, pink legs!
The little duckling is very pleased.

The little duckling sees an eagle.
'What beautiful wings! I want beautiful wings, too!'
Suddenly, the little duckling has big, brown wings!

The little duckling is very pleased.

The little duckling sees a cock.
'What a beautiful hat! I want a beautiful hat, too!'
Suddenly, the little duckling has a big, red, handsome hat!
The little duckling is very pleased.

All the little duckling's friends swim in the river.
The little duckling says, 'Stop! Wait for me!'
And he jumps into the water.
But his peacock's tail is very heavy.
His big, brown wings are very heavy.
His long, thin, pink legs cannot swim.
His handsome red hat is very heavy and he can't breathe.
'Glug! Glug! Glug!
I want a little duckling's tail, and a little duckling's legs and wings, and I don't want a hat!'

Suddenly the little duckling can swim. And he can swim very well. Soon he is with his friends.

COMMENTS

The correct technical term for a cock's 'hat' is 'comb'. I have used 'hat' here and in 3.8 as it looks like a hat and this term is easier for children to learn and use.

The little duckling: lesson plan

LEVEL

Beginners

AGE

8 to 10

TIME

30 minutes

LANGUAGE

Complimenting: *What a beautiful hat!*; *I want/don't want . . .*; adjectives; animals

PREPARATION

Find or draw pictures of a peacock, a flamingo, an eagle, and a cock.

IN CLASS

1 Show the illustrations on a poster or give each pair a copy of the pictures which go with this story. Talk about the peacock, getting the children to say whatever they can.

2 Tell the children the first verse of the story. Mime it as dramatically as you can.
If you want the children to see the written word then write this first verse on the board.

3 See if the children can predict the next verse (with the flamingo), then tell it.

4 See if the children can predict the next verse (with the eagle), then tell it.

5 See if the children can predict the next verse (with the cock), then tell it.

6 Tell and mime the verse which describes the little duckling sinking. Get the children all to chorus the last line, 'I want a little duckling's tail, and a little duckling's legs and wings, and I don't want a hat!'

7 Tell and mime the last part of the story.

FOLLOW-UP 1

The children work in groups, each group making a poster of one of the verses.

FOLLOW-UP 2

The children work in pairs to make a new verse. Note: they only have to find the word for an animal and then the word for its most noticeable feature. For example, elephant–trunk; giraffe–neck; shark–fin/teeth.

FOLLOW-UP 3

The idea of the suitability of the design of animals or objects for their purpose is one you and the children might follow up in relation to this story.

Animals: kangaroos, crocodiles, rabbits, turtles.

Objects: family cars, racing cars, chairs, beds, houses, shops.

Why are they well designed?

What would happen if you used them for something else?

COMMENTS

1 This version of the story is very much about design and function – the little duckling is perfectly designed to swim about on the water with his friends. Long, thin legs are meant for walking about in the water, and broad eagle's wings are meant for gliding on wind currents.

2 The better-known version of this story is the same as this version until he has the tail, legs, wings and cock's comb. Then, in the better-known version, all the animals laugh at the little duckling saying how foolish he looks. The little ducking is ashamed and wishes he looks like all the other little ducklings again. You might discuss this with older children; the idea of laughing at someone for wanting to be different but not harming anyone.

Elementary

3.4 The little Indian boy

Story	Instructions
The little Indian boy wakes up.	*Open your eyes and yawn.*
He gets out of bed.	*Step out and stretch.*
He gets dressed.	*Pull on a shirt.*
He has his breakfast.	*Eat and drink.*
He says to his mummy, 'Oooooooooooooooooo! I'm going to play.'	
He walks down the garden path, walk, whistle, walk, whistle, walk, whistle.	*Walk and whistle.*
He opens and closes the green gate. Click!	*Open the gate, go through it, and close it.*
There's a twisty road.	*Point.*
He walks down the twisty road, walk, whistle, walk, whistle.	*Walk and whistle.*
There's a dark wood.	*Point.*
He goes into the dark wood, quietly. Sh! Sh! Sh! Sh! Sh! Sh!	*Finger on lips, moving head to each side.*
He walks through the dark wood, tip, toe, tip, toe, tip, toe.	*Walk on tiptoe, swinging your body.*
There's some tall grass.	*Point.*
He walks through the tall grass, swish, swish, swish, swish, swish.	*Part the tall grass with your hands.*
There's some wet mud.	*Point.*
He walks through the wet mud, suck, squelch, suck, squelch, suck, squelch.	*Lift your feet as if pulling them up out of sticky mud (or your hands if you are imitating walking with them).*
There's a deep river!	*Point.*
He swims across the deep river swim, swim, swim, swim, swim, swim.	*Swim with your hands and arms.*

There's a steep hill.	*Point.*
He climbs the steep hill, gasp, gasp, gasp, gasp, gasp, gasp.	*Swing from side to side and gasp.*
There's a cave! It's a very dark cave!	*Point.*
He looks into the dark cave, peep, peep, peep, peep, peep, peep.	*Look from side to side.*
He listens.	*Several seconds of silence in which your eyes move from side to side.*
Nothing.	*Say it in an expressive whisper.*
He goes into the dark cave, creep, creep, creep, creep, creep, creep.	*Creep or make your hands creep if you are imitating feet with them.*
Deeper and deeper and deeper, and deeper and deeper and deeper, into the dark cave . . .	*Speak slowly in a whisper and creep.*
Suddenly!	*Open your eyes wide and look frightened.*
Grrrrrrrrrrrrrrrrrrrrrrrrrr!	*Say it loudly and tremble at the same time.*
A lion!	*Shout.*
The little Indian boy runs out of the cave, pitter, patter, pitter, patter, pitter, patter.	*Say it quickly. Run or imitate running with your hands.*
Down the hill, stumble, stagger, stumble, stagger, stumble, stagger.	*Stagger from side to side with your body.*
Across the river, swim, swim, swim, swim, swim, swim.	*Swim with your hands.*
Through the mud, suck, squelch, suck, squelch, suck, squelch.	*Walk in sticky mud.*
Through the grass, swish, swish, swish, swish, swish, swish.	*Part the tall grass with your hands.*
Through the wood, tip, toe, tip, toe, tip, toe.	*Run on tiptoe swinging your body.*
Up the road, run, run, run, run, run, run.	*Arms swinging with running action.*

Open the gate, close the gate, click!	*Open and close the gate.*
Up the garden path, run, run, run, run, run, run.	*Make a running action.*
Open the door, close the door, bang!	*Open and close the door.* *Slap a table very hard.*
'Don't bang the door!' says his mum. 'Ooooooooooooooooooooooo! Mum!'	

The little Indian boy: lesson plan

The children learn a rhythmic text combined with dramatic body movement.

LEVEL

Elementary

AGE

8 to 12

TIME

35 minutes

LANGUAGE

Simple present tense; prepositions; adjectives; contrasting definite and indefinite articles

PREPARATION

1 Find a feather and a headband to stick it in. If possible have a feather and headband for everyone. The children can make them out of paper or thin card.

2 Draw a large map of where the little Indian boy goes or be ready to draw it on the board (see page 87).

3 Write out the whole story on a large sheet (or sheets) of paper large enough for it to be legible from a distance.

IN CLASS

1 Display the map you have made or begin to draw it on the board. Make sure that the children know the words *garden, garden path, gate, road, wood, grass, mud, river, hill, cave*.

2 Tell the children to bring their chairs into a semicircle around you if possible. If they remain in their places they should clear their desks and have nothing in their hands or on their laps.

3 Choose a child you know will be able to co-operate with you by acting. Put the headband and feather on his or her head. Lay him down on a table. Tell the class he is asleep.

4 Now manipulate the 'little Indian boy' as if he were a puppet: make him wake up, get out of bed, pretend to pull on a shirt, have his breakfast, and at the same time you say the lines of text up to the sentence *I'm going to play*.

down the
garden path

through the
wet mud

opens and
closes the gate

across the
deep river

down the
twisty road

up the
steep hill

into the
dark wood

into the
dark cave

through the
dark wood

out of the
dark cave

through the
high grass

down the
steep hill

Say the first four lines and then teach the class to say:

Oooooooooooooooooo!
I'm going to play!

5 Now take off the headband and feather so that the 'little Indian boy' is an ordinary child again and ask him to sit down in the semicircle with the others (or give everyone a headband and feather). Say, 'We are all little Indian boys or girls now. Do what I do, but this first time, don't speak.'

6 Tell and act the whole story now as far as the cave. Get the children to act it with you. In order for this to be successful you must spend time on each action and go very slowly. If you are worried about forgetting the story then use the large sheet you have prepared and display it where you can see it easily. But you may find that the map is enough of a prompt.

7 Act and tell the story again. This time make sure that all the children are doing the actions with you in time to the rhythm you are setting.

8 Act and tell it again, but this time invite the children to say as much of the text as they can with you. Do this several times until most of the class have got it right.

9 Ask the children to imagine what is in the cave.

10 Continue the story to the end in the same way.

FOLLOW-UP 1   Once the children know the story and actions they can walk around in a large circle, one behind the other, speaking and acting.

FOLLOW-UP 2   The children can draw the map in their books and either write out the whole story or just note down the words and phrases they liked (or you might want them to concentrate on the prepositions).

FOLLOW-UP 3   Take the same idea of a story based on a journey through sensations and make up a new one with the children. You can keep to the same lines and only change the individual words. Possibilities might be a journey through the school or through a town.

COMMENTS   You might find it helpful to write the text out on a large wallchart. Alternatively, you might teach a much reduced version the first few times and then keep adding verses as the children master the ones you have given them.

3.5 Father, son, and donkey

A father and his son take their donkey to the market.

A man says, 'You are stupid! Why do you walk? You can ride the donkey!'

So the father gets on the donkey.

A woman says, 'You are not very kind. You ride on the donkey and your little boy walks!'
So the father gets off the donkey and his son gets on the donkey.

A man says, 'You are not very nice to your father! You ride and he walks!'
So the father gets on the donkey and sits behind his son.

A woman says, 'Is that your donkey? Are you crazy? Two people? You are very heavy! The donkey is nearly dead.'
So the father and son get off the donkey.

A man says, 'Are you going to the market? Then carry the donkey! It is very tired!'
So the father and his son carry the donkey to the market.

In the market everybody laughs! They don't want to buy the donkey!
'It's a very lazy donkey! You are carrying it to the market!'
So the father and his son and the donkey walk home again.

If you try to make everybody happy you will make nobody happy.

Father, son, and donkey: lesson plan

LEVEL	**Elementary**
AGE	**8 to 12+**
TIME	**45 minutes with another 30 minutes for the dramatization**
LANGUAGE	**Oral fluency through retelling and dramatization; listening skills**
PREPARATION	**1** Select the words which are important for the story and new for the children.

1 Select the words which are important for the story and new for the children.

2 Practise the story to make sure you can tell it from memory.

3 Make a photocopy of page 90 for each child or pair (if possible on to card).

4 Make an example of the figures on page 90 to use while telling the story. All the figures can be carried by each other as in the story.

IN CLASS

Before the story

1 Tell the children that you are going to tell them a story, but do not give them the title at this point. Then tell them that you are going to teach them some important words so that they can understand the story easily.

2 Say, for example, *This story is about a man, a boy, and their donkey. Who knows what a donkey is?* Teach new words by drawing, showing pictures, miming, or demonstrating.

3 Put each new word into a sentence (orally only).

4 Then ask the children to show whether they have understood the word by saying it in their mother tongue.

5 Finally, write the English word and the mother-tongue equivalent on the board (or on prepared word card strips complete with pictures).

6 Then say, *The name of the story is 'Father, son, and donkey'.* You can write the title of the story on the board if you wish.

During the story

7 Tell the story without a book, standing and acting out the parts.

8 Use the figures from page 90 to illustrate the story and highlight the humour in it.

After the story

9 Ask questions to find out if the children have understood the main points of the story. Ask the class to retell the story, each child telling one or two sentences.

10 The children make models of the characters by cutting out the figures on page 90 and sticking them on to card. They use them to retell the story to each other.

11 Finish by dramatizing the story with the children. If you are only going to do the dramatization once, get all the children to take part. There are eight main parts, plus a crowd of people at the market. Some children could be trees or other inanimate objects. If you are going to dramatize the story more than once then only use enough children for the protagonists of the story. The rest of the class watch and this is beneficial for all concerned.

You narrate the story and prompt the sentences the children should say, i.e. say the sentence and they repeat it. The more able children often remember the sentences, particularly those which are repeated again and again in the story.

Ask the children to get into character before you begin, for example, ask the child playing the donkey to walk about in the way he or she thinks a donkey walks.

FOLLOW-UP 1 The children call out phrases or sentences from any part of the story and you write them on the board, in any order. The children then write the sentences in the correct sequence in their books.

FOLLOW-UP 2 The children call out phrases or sentences and you write them on the board. The children then copy one of the sentences and illustrate it.

FOLLOW-UP 3 The children make a book of the story based on the sentences compiled in either of the two activities above.

COMMENTS The chief aim is to develop listening skills with children in the first two years of learning English. The sequence as described can be applied to most stories but of course it will need adaptation. For example, here I have suggested that you make a cardboard cut-out of the boy, his father, and the donkey because it adds visual humour in this particular story. As a general rule, Aliza Irene Handler does not show pictures of the whole story to help with meaning because she pre-teaches key words and wants to encourage children to use their imagination.

Acknowledgements

This lesson plan was devised by Aliza Irene Handler, who is a classroom teacher, teacher trainer, and professional storyteller.

3.6 The little white cat

Once upon a time there was a little white cat. This little white cat has six brothers and sisters. They are all black and her mother and father are black. The little white cat doesn't know that she is white. She thinks she is black, too.

The little white cat grows older and older and bigger and bigger. One day the little white cat says, 'Do I want to be a farmer? No. Do I want to be a teacher? No. I know—I want to be a witch's cat!'

So the little white cat says to her mum, 'Goodbye, mum! I'm going to be a witch's cat!'
'Oh, that's nice!' says the little white cat's mum.
'Goodbye! Come and see us soon.'

The little white cat looks for a witch. She walks and she walks and she walks. At last she finds a witch.
'Hello, witch. Have you got a cat?'
'No, I haven't got a cat.'
'Well, I'm your cat!' says the little white cat.

'No, you're not! You're white. Witches have black cats. Go away!'

The poor little white cat! She is so sad! But she looks for another witch, and she walks and she walks and she walks. At last she finds another witch.
'Hello, witch. Have you got a cat?'
'No, I haven't got a cat.'
'Well, I'm your cat!' says the little white cat.
'No, you're not! You're white. Witches have black cats. Go away!'

The poor little white cat! She is so sad and so hungry. She hasn't got a job. She hasn't got any money. She hasn't got any food. She is so hungry and so weak. But she looks for another witch and so she walks and she walks and she walks.

At last she comes to a cottage. There is a chimney sweep sitting behind the cottage. He is eating his lunch, sandwiches and cake.
'Hello, you are a poor little cat. What's wrong?'
'I'm so weak, I'm so hungry. I haven't got a job and I haven't got any money.'
'Well, here's a sandwich.'
'Thank you!' says the little white cat.
The little white cat eats the sandwich and then she feels better and stronger.

Then she looks at the chimney sweep's bag of black, black soot. She puts in her paw. She looks at her paw. It's so black! She puts in her leg. She looks at her leg. It's so black! She jumps into the bag and then she jumps out of the bag.
'You are so black! Now you are a little black cat!'
'Am I? Am I a black cat? That's good because I'm going to be a witch's cat!'
'You're lucky! You're so lucky! This is a witch's cottage! She is sitting in the rocking chair in the front door!'
The little white cat—the little black cat—walks around the house to the front door. There is the witch sitting on her rocking chair in the sunshine. Her eyes are closed.

'Hello. Have you got a cat?'
'No, I haven't got a cat.'
'Well, I'm your cat!' says the little white cat.

'Oh, that's nice! Jump on my knee. Oh, you are a nice little cat!' The witch strokes the little white cat—the little black cat. Then she says, 'What a pity, I can't see you because I'm blind.'

COMMENTS

I was told this story by the great Scottish traditional storyteller, Duncan Williamson. This version of the story is not exactly as Duncan told it to me. I have adapted it to make it more easily understood for the young learner of English. I have also made the cat 'she' rather than 'he' so that girls are brought up with the idea that they can go out into the world and explore it just like boys.

witch

brush

broom

cottage

brush

sandwich

chimney sweep

bag of soot

The little white cat: lesson plan

The children listen to a story, listen to it again, and act it out, then listen again and act it and speak the parts. The technique will work with most short stories in which there are three to six people who have a speaking part.

LEVEL	**Elementary**
AGE	**7 to 10**
TIME	**35 minutes**
LANGUAGE	**Listening and some speaking; *have you got . . . ?*, *have/haven't got*; introductions; adjectives**
MATERIALS	A large piece of paper (for example, A2) and a thick black felt tip pen.
PREPARATION	1 You must know your story by heart or read it from a text.
	2 Learn how to draw, a cat, a witch, a chimney sweep, and a cottage. Use the drawings on page 94 as a model. See also Chapter 7, page 207.
IN CLASS	1 Introduce the children to the little white cat and to her parents and brothers and sisters by drawing them on a large piece of paper (not the board because you can keep the drawing you make on paper and use it again). Then draw the three witches, the chimney sweep, and the cottage. Explain the job of a sweep: he doesn't sweep the floor (mime), he sweeps the chimney (mime and point to the chimney of the cottage). Tell the children there are six main characters in the story (the little white cat, the cat's mother, witch 1, witch 2, witch 3, chimney sweep).
	2 Divide the children into groups of six or less. If there are fewer children in one of the groups then one child can play two of the six characters, for example, a witch and the sweep. Explain to the children, before you put them into groups, what is going to happen. You are going to tell them a story several times. All they have to do the *first* time is listen.
	The *second* time they listen and mime a character.
	The *third* time they listen, act a character, and say some words the character says.
	3 First telling: Make the story as understandable as you can through acting and through pictures. The children only listen.
	4 Second telling: Ask the children in each group to divide the characters between them. They should then introduce themselves to each other. If you wish they can walk around the classroom introducing themselves to other children in the class. Tell them to stand up and to mime their character as you tell the story.

5 Third telling: Ask the children to try to say some of the words of their character as you tell the story. You will have to allow time for the children to do this—basically the children repeat what you say when it is their character speaking. The same character from each group should do their acting and speaking at the same time.

FOLLOW-UP

1 Record the play on audio cassette, and perform it with puppets, with shadow puppets, etc.

FOLLOW-UP

2 Make a book of the story.

3.7 Little Red Riding Hood

Little Red Riding Hood's mother says, 'Little Red Riding Hood! Come here. Take this basket to your grandmother. There are sandwiches and there is a cake in the basket. Be careful! There is a wolf in the forest and he is very dangerous.'

Little Red Riding Hood walks in the forest. There are many big trees and beautiful flowers in the forest and the birds are singing. Little Red Riding Hood likes flowers and she picks them. She doesn't see the wolf hiding behind the tree. The wolf is thinking!

The wolf meets Little Red Riding Hood. He says, 'Hello.'
'Hello,' says Little Red Riding Hood.
'Where are you going?' asks the wolf.
'I'm going to my grandmother's cottage.'
'Oh! Where does she live?'
'She lives in a cottage in the forest.'
'That's nice. OK. Goodbye. See you later.'
'Bye-bye!'
'Bye-bye!'

The wolf runs to Grandmother's cottage. He knocks on the door.
'Who's that?' says Grandmother.
'It's me!'
'Who's me?'
'It's Little Red Riding Hood!' says the wolf.
'Come in, dear!'

The wolf goes into the cottage and eats Grandmother. The wolf gets into bed. He waits for Little Red Riding Hood. He is hungry!

Little Red Riding Hood dances and sings in the forest. At last she comes to her grandmother's cottage.

She knocks on the door. 'Who's that?' says the wolf.

'It's me.'

'Who's me?'

'It's Little Red Riding Hood,' says Little Red Riding Hood.

'Come in, my dear.'

Little Red Riding Hood goes into the cottage.

She looks at the wolf in bed. 'What big ears you've got, Grandmother!'

'I want to hear you, my dear,' says the wolf.

'What big eyes you've got, Grandmother!'

'I want to see you, my dear.'

'What big teeth you've got, Grandmother!'

'I want to eat you, my dear!'

The wolf jumps out of bed and eats Little Red Riding Hood.

A man comes. He has an axe. He kills the wolf. Grandmother and Little Red Riding Hood jump out of the wolf.

Little Red Riding Hood: lesson plan 1

LEVEL	**Elementary and for those who have begun reading in their own language**
AGE	**8 to 12**
TIME	**60 minutes**
LANGUAGE	**Listening and reading fluency: being able to skim through a text and get a general idea of its meaning**
PREPARATION	**1** Photocopy the picture strip on page 98 and the text of the story on page 99. Make enough copies for one per group of four or five children. Remember you can photocopy directly on to card.
	2 Glue the picture strip on to card and cut it up into separate pictures. Cut up the text and glue the relevant bits of the text onto the backs of the pictures. Remember to cut off the sentence numbers!
	3 Practise drawing the sketches in Step 1.

LITTLE RED RIDING HOOD	
1	Take this basket to your grandmother.
2	The wolf meets Little Red Riding Hood.
3	The wolf runs to Grandmother's cottage.
4	The wolf gets into bed.
5	Little Red Riding Hood comes to her grandmother's cottage.
6	She looks at the wolf in bed.
7	The wolf jumps out of bed and eats Little Red Riding Hood.
8	A man comes and kills the wolf.

Photocopiable © Oxford University Press

IN CLASS

1 Draw Little Red Riding Hood on the board. If you are not very good at drawing that is all the better! Here are some drawings to help you:

2 Ask:

You: *Who's this?*

Children: *It's* (Little Red Riding Hood *in mother tongue*)

You: *Yes, that's right. In English she's called Little Red Riding Hood.*

If they don't recognize her, you can draw the wolf, the forest, the little house, and the grandmother. Keep on asking who she/he/it is. Give the children the words *wolf, forest, house, grandmother.*
If you want to explain the reason for Little Red Riding Hood's name in English, say that she has a kind of cloak (riding hood) which she wears all the time, so people call her after it. But point out that she doesn't ride a horse.

3 To find out if the children know the story, ask them to tell it to you as a class. A rudimentary telling is enough, for example:

Children: *It's a girl. She goes to her grandmother. A wolf eats her grandmother. The wolf eats Little Red Riding Hood. A man comes. He kills the wolf.*

4 Put the children in groups of three to four, sitting around a table so that they can all see the pictures the right way up. Give each group a set of pictures.

5 Tell the groups to sort out the pictures and put them into their correct order. When they have finished, let them walk about looking at how neighbouring groups sequenced them to see if they have done it in the same way.

6 Tell the children the story and let them follow it in their sequence of pictures.

7 Tell the children to mix up their pictures and then to turn them over to see the words on the other side.

8 Tell them now to try to put the texts in order. Ask them not to look at the pictures but to do it by getting the general idea from each bit of text.

9 When they have done their best to put the texts in order they can turn the cards over to show the pictures and see if they have put the texts in the correct order.

10 Tell the children to turn back to the texts and then tell them the story again. If you tell the text rather than read it there will be more challenge for the pupils to listen for the gist of what you are saying rather than to follow what you are saying word by word, merely recognizing the sound–spelling relationship.

COMMENTS

The story of Little Red Riding Hood is very useful in language teaching for several reasons:
- It is well-known so the children can concentrate on recognizing the story rather than trying to wrestle meaning out of a new story.
- There are four characters in the story and several locations which help to give it variety.

– In recent years several authors have enjoyed re-writing Little Red Riding Hood, notably James Thurber and Roald Dahl.

For all these reasons I did not want to omit it from this collection!

Little Red Riding Hood: lesson plan 2

LEVEL	**Elementary or even beginners**
AGE	**Any**
TIME	**30 minutes**
LANGUAGE	**Listening and speaking fluency**
IN CLASS	**1** Tell the class the story of Little Red Riding Hood.

2 With the whole class, help the children retell the story. As they do so, write on the board the key parts of the story, for example:

Mother and Little Red Riding Hood
Little Red Riding Hood and the wolf
Wolf and Grandma
Wolf and Little Red Riding Hood

3 Say *Who am I?* Then say a sentence spoken by one of the characters in the story. If it is a sentence spoken more than once and by different characters you must imitate the way of saying it so that the children can guess who you are. For example:

You: *Who's that?* (said in a very evil way plus a bit of suppressed crazy laughter).
Class: *The wolf!*

4 The children walk about in a large area. Ask them to walk about and to think quietly about the story. Ask them to stop and 'freeze' every so often and to think about a particular part of the story. Ask them to walk about again but then to stop and this time to think about a particular character in that same position. They should move about as if they are that person or character (for example, the wolf).

5 They stop and think about one key moment in the story from that character's point of view. They should ask themselves what their character did, said, or might have said. They should think of one sentence.

6 Then they walk about and say their sentence to other children as they meet them. They should try to act it in character.

7 After some time let the children respond to each other in character and say anything they wish.

This is a general description of what can be done with most
stories which have a number of characters in them.

3.8 Ma Liang

Ma Liang is a Chinese girl and she loves drawing but she is very
poor and she hasn't got a brush. Ma Liang draws her pictures on
the ground. She draws with a stick.

One day she closes her eyes and she says three times, 'I want a
brush! I want a brush! I want a brush!'

Ma Liang opens her eyes and there, in front of her, is an old
man. He has got a long white beard and he is holding a brush.

The old man says, 'This brush is for you!'
'For me?'
'Yes, it's for you. Take it! It's yours!'
'It's mine?'
'Yes, it's yours! It's for you!'

Ma Liang takes the brush and she looks at it. It is a beautiful
brush. She wants to say 'Thank you'. But the old man isn't
there! Ma Liang looks in front of her; he isn't there. She looks
to the right; he isn't there. She looks to the left; he isn't there.
She looks behind her; he isn't there.

Ma Liang finds a piece of paper. 'What can I draw?'

Then she sees a cock so she draws a cock.

'Here's its head. Here's its handsome hat. Here's its bright eye.
Here's its proud neck. Here's its strong body. Here are its long,
strong legs. And here are its long tail feathers.'

Suddenly, the picture begins to move. The cock is standing up
on the paper! It is a real cock! Then it jumps off the paper and it
runs away!

'Wonderful! It's a magic brush!'

'What can I draw now? I know, a hen!'
'Here's its red hat and here's its head. Here's its bright eye.
Here's its fat neck and fat body. Here are its legs and its feet.'

Suddenly, the picture begins to move. The hen is standing up on
the paper! It is a real hen!
Ma Liang picks up the hen and goes to a little house. The
woman in the house is very poor. She hasn't got any hens. Ma
Liang says, 'This hen is for you.'
'For me?'
'Yes, it's for you. Take it. It's yours.'
'It's mine?'
'Yes, it's yours. It's for you.'

The hen lays an egg. The poor old woman is very happy!

Then Ma Liang sees an old man. He is trying to cut some sticks.
But his axe is very old.
Ma Liang draws an axe: a new, shiny, sharp axe.
Suddenly, the axe begins to move. There it is, on the paper! Ma
Liang takes the axe to the old man.
'This axe is for you.'
'For me?'
'Yes, it's for you. Take it. It's yours.'
'It's mine?'
'Yes, it's yours. It's for you.'

The old man cuts the sticks. He is very happy.

Then Ma Liang sees a farmer. He is trying to pull a plough in
his field.
Ma Liang draws a cow: a big, strong cow.
'Here's its small head and big gentle eye. Here's its short, strong
neck and its long, strong body. Here are its short, strong legs.'
Suddenly, the cow begins to move. It stands up on the paper and
then it jumps on to the ground and it begins to grow, bigger and
bigger and bigger. Ma Liang takes the cow to the farmer.
'This cow is for you.'
'For me?'
'Yes, it's for you. Take it. It's yours.'
'It's mine?'
'Yes, it's yours. It's for you.'

The cow pulls the plough. The farmer is very happy!

Everybody in the village knows Ma Liang. She draws things for
all the poor people.

One day two soldiers come to the village. 'Where is Ma Liang?'
The people in the village say, 'She's there! That's Ma Liang! She
is our wonderful girl!'
'Are you Ma Liang?'
'Yes.'
'The king wants you. Come with us.'
'Why?'
'The king wants a picture.'
'No, I won't come! I won't draw a picture for the king! He has
got a palace, and soldiers, farms and horses, and a lot of money!
No, I won't come!'

The two soldiers take Ma Liang to the king. The king is in the
garden.
'Are you Ma Liang?'
'Yes.'
'Have you got your brush?'
'Yes.'
'Draw me a tree. Draw a tree for me! Draw me a tree, full of
golden coins!'

'No, no, I won't! I won't draw a tree! I won't draw a tree, full of golden coins.'
'Draw me a tree. Draw a tree for me! Draw me a tree, full of golden coins!'
'No, no, I won't! I won't draw a tree! I won't draw a tree, full of golden coins.'
'Put her in prison!'

Ma Liang is in prison. What can she do?
Ma Liang draws a key, a big key for the door of the prison.
She puts the key in the lock. She turns the key. She opens the door. She looks into the corridor. She sees some soldiers. She walks slowly and quietly down the corridor. Suddenly, the soldiers see her! 'Hey! You! Stop! Come back!' 'Hey! You! Stop! Come back!'

Ma Liang begins to run. The soldiers begin to run. What can she do?

Ma Liang draws a horse! She jumps on the horse and the horse begins to run. The soldiers and the king jump on their horses and they begin to run!

Ma Liang's horse is very fast. But the king and the soldiers get nearer and nearer and nearer.

What can Ma Liang do?

Ma Liang draws a hole! She throws the hole on the ground behind her. The hole grows bigger and bigger and bigger. The king and all the soldiers and their horses run into the hole!

Ma Liang walks slowly back home to her village. The people are very happy! They love Ma Liang.

COMMENTS

The correct technical term for a cock's 'hat' is 'comb'—see 3.3, 'The little duckling', page 81.

Ma Liang: lesson plan

LEVEL Elementary

AGE 8 to 12

TIME Two 45-minute lessons

LANGUAGE

Listening; new vocabulary and structures; possessive pronouns; *Would* and *if* clauses; speaking fluency; reading and writing

MATERIALS

If possible, a Chinese-style brush and ink stick.

PREPARATION

1 Make photocopies of the pictures of the story on page 106 for each pair and cut them up. You might like to photocopy enlargements of the pictures for use on the board.

2 Make picture word cards (pictures on one side and the word on the other) of the new important words in the story which the children do not know, for example, *brush*.

3 Prepare a gapped story (see page 38). If you have time make several different versions of the gaps. Make enough copies for each group of two or three children.

4 Prepare slips of paper with one or two sentences on them describing actions in the story. Make enough for each child to have one.

5 Write out some important parts of the story in verse form. The sentences should encourage a rhythmic chanting to take place. For examples, see page 109.

IN CLASS

Before the story

1 All the children are standing. Say, 'You can sit down if you have got. . . . ' (a bag, a pen, a jacket, a book, etc.). This practises a structure in the story.

2 Now ask several children to lend you some objects, and put them into a box on your table. Make sure everybody sees what you have taken. Keep on referring to *Peter's pen . . . it's Peter's . . . it's his/yours*, etc. Put your hand into the box and hold one of the objects.

Now I've got something in my hand. What is it?
Child: *It's a book!*
You: *No.*
Child: *It's a key.*
You: *Whose key is it?*
Child: *It's Wendy's.*
You: *Yes. It's Wendy's. Here, Wendy. Take it. It's yours.*

Do this with each object, thus practising possessive forms which are a key part of the story.

3 Say:
I'm going to tell you a story. The story is about a girl. Her name is Ma Liang. Ma Liang is Chinese. She lives in China. Ma Liang likes drawing and painting pictures. But she is very poor and she wants something. What does she want?
The children guess.

4 Draw a series of steps for each letter of PAINT BRUSH. Ask the children to guess what the letters and the word might be.

Children: *Is there a letter 's' in the word?*
You: *Yes, here it is.*

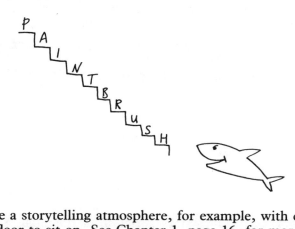

5 Create a storytelling atmosphere, for example, with cushions on the floor to sit on. See Chapter 1, page 16, for more suggestions on this.

During the story

6 First telling: Help the children's understanding with mime, acting, and drawing.

7 When you have told the story, put the children into pairs and hand out the cut-up pictures of the story. Do a quick retelling with the children's help. At the same time, the children put the pictures into the correct order according to the story. Then sequence your large pictures, sticking them to the board, with the children's help.

8 Second telling: Give each child a picture or word card. The children should hold their cards up when they hear their word in the story. They should also imitate your actions, gestures, and mimes, and make noises, sound effects, etc.

9 Third telling: The children repeat the key phrases after you, clapping to the rhythm, chanting with different emotions, sometimes loudly and sometimes quietly, etc. See page 109 for examples.

After the story

10 You retell the story but make a lot of mistakes. Tell them you are tired and make fun of yourself! When the children hear a mistake they must put up their hands, clap, stand up, or stamp their feet. They then correct you.

11 The children then retell the story with the help of the sequence of pictures on the board.

12 Give out copies of the gapped story. The children complete it in groups. If you have made several versions of the gaps then the children can go to other groups and check the words and copy the words which are missing from their own text.

13 Give each child a slip of paper with a sentence or two describing an action in the story. The children should try to mime their action. The other children should guess what it is. Note: all the children now have a complete copy of the story.

FOLLOW-UP 1

This story is rich in its potential. You could go on to study where China is and what the countryside is like. You might get hold of a book of Chinese paintings and an actual Chinese or Japanese brush with its dry stick of black ink which must be mixed with water. The Chinese keep their brushes vertical when painting and it would be interesting to try to do this.

FOLLOW-UP 2

Do a topic study of the basic things that people need in life and make a collage of children's pictures or cut out magazine pictures of these.

FOLLOW-UP 3

Invent and write some new stories about Ma Liang.

FOLLOW-UP 4

Write some new variations of the chants, for example:

Draw a tree!
No, I won't draw a tree!
Draw a house!
No, I won't draw a house!
Draw a mouse!
No, I won't draw a mouse!

Acknowledgements

This lesson plan was devised by Eva Benkö for her class of 11- to 12-year-olds.

COMMENTS

Eva Benkö comments: I do not expect my children to be familiar with all the language they hear me use or all the language they will hear and read in the story. This is quite demanding on my children because there are no cognates or even similar words in

English and Hungarian. Nevertheless, I don't think it is a problem for them. In this activity the children learn the story and chant parts of it.

Ma Liang: verses for choral chanting

This brush* is for you! (*hen, cow, axe)

For me?

Yes, it's for you. Take it! It's yours!

It's mine?

Yes, it's yours! It's for you!

Draw me a tree. Draw a tree for me! Draw me a tree, full of golden coins!

No, no, I won't! I won't draw a tree! I won't draw a tree, full of golden coins!

Draw me a tree. Draw a tree for me! Draw me a tree, full of golden coins!

No, no, I won't! I won't draw a tree! I won't draw a tree, full of golden coins!

Photocopiable © Oxford University Press

VARIATIONS

I can't get out!
She can't get out!
I want to be free!
She wants to be free!
What can I do?
What can she do?
I can draw a key!
She can draw a key!

Draw me a tree!
Draw a tree for me!
Draw me a tree,
Full of golden coins!
No, no, I won't!
I won't draw a tree!
I won't draw a tree,
Full of golden coins!

Draw a tree!
No, I won't! I won't draw a tree!
Draw a house!
No, I won't! I won't draw a house!
Draw a mouse!
No, I won't draw a mouse!

Acknowledgements

Carolyn Graham is widely acknowledged as the main disseminator of the power of chanting everyday phrases. But I also have to thank Carolyn Laidlaw for her demonstration of chanting variations in the Ma Liang story. It is a coincidence that Eva Benkö, the originator of these teacher's notes, also uses rhythmic chanting techniques. It all goes to show how useful they are!

3.9 The prince and the dragon

1 A prince comes to town.
All the people say, 'He's beautiful!'
The prince says, 'I kill dragons.'
'Dragons?' say all the people.
'Dragons!' says the prince.

2 'We've got a dragon!'
'You've got a dragon. YOU'VE GOT A DRAGON?!!!'
'We've got a dragon and it eats a princess every day.'
'It eats a princess every day?'
'Kill the dragon and you can have the last princess!' says the king.
'Kill the dragon and I can have the last princess?'

3 'It lives in the lake. Let's go!'
'It lives in the lake?'
The prince goes to the lake with the king and all the people.
'This is the lake!' says the king.
'This is the lake?'

4 'And this is the last princess.'
'The last princess?'
'Hello.'
'Hello.'

5 'Now I can hear the dragon,' says the king.
'Uuurrrrrrrrrummmmmmmeeeeeekkkkkk!
Uuurrrrrrrrrummmmmmmeeeeeekkkkkk!
Uuurrrrrrrrrummmmmmmeeeeeekkkkkk!
Uuurrrrrrrrrummmmmmmeeeeeekkkkkk!'
'Yes, that's the dragon.'
'That's the dragon?'

6 'Yes, the dragon is coming and we are going,' say the king and the people.
'We are going?'
'Not you, us!' say the king and the people.
'We are staying,' says the princess.
'Staying?'

7 'Uuurrrrrrrrrummmmmmmeeeeeekkkkkk!
Uuurrrrrrrrrummmmmmmeeeeeekkkkkk!
Uuurrrrrrrrrummmmmmmeeeeeekkkkkk!
Uuurrrrrrrrrummmmmmmeeeeeekkkkkk!'
'This is the dragon.'
'The dragon?'
'Kill it and I am your princess.'
'Kill it?!!!'

8 'Uuurrrrrrrrrummmmmmmeeeeeekkkkkk!
Uuurrrrrrrrrummmmmmmeeeeeekkkkkk!'
'Do you kill dragons?' asks the princess. 'Yes or no?'
'Do I kill dragons?' asks the prince.
'Yes.'
'No.'

9 So the dragon eats the princess.
'Uughhh!' says the dragon.
'Uughhh?' says the prince.

The prince and the dragon: lesson plan

This must be one of the most gentle entries into a story possible!
Essentially, you tell the story in the mother tongue, and the children illustrate the story and work out which words in English they will need to tell it.

LEVEL   **Beginners to elementary**

AGE   **6 to 10**

TIME	**80 minutes**
LANGUAGE	**General listening fluency plus oral and written accuracy of one or two sentences**
PREPARATION	You can make a giant picture strip sequence by using large sheets of paper for each group of three children. Alternatively, get a long length of wallpaper or get a left-over roll of paper from the printers of a local newspaper.

The story of 'The prince and the dragon' divides conveniently into nine parts. If you have about 30 children you may want to organize the production of two stories or have more children in each group.

IN CLASS

1 Tell the story of 'The prince and the dragon' in the children's mother tongue, or get them to retell a story they know about a dragon.

2 Discuss with the class how the story could be divided up. I have suggested nine divisions or scenes, but you and the children may not want to do it this way.
Summarize on the board in the mother tongue (unless the children can cope with it in English) each part of the story you have decided on, for example:

Part 1: The prince arrives in town.
Part 2: The people say there is a dragon.
Part 3: They go to the lake.

3 Agree with the children which three children take which part. Each three should then do a large picture showing their part of the story. The long roll of paper must be stretched out on the floor to work on. You should measure off about one metre per group of three. As the children work, talk to them about what they are doing—as much as you judge to be appropriate in English. This will begin to introduce to them the words that they will need.

4 When the picture strip is ready, display it so that everybody can see it easily. Tell the story again in the mother tongue.

5 Now ask the children to write down all the English words they can think of that they might need to tell the part of the story illustrated by their picture.

6 Ask the children to write down all the words in their mother tongue that they don't know in English but will need to tell their part of the story.

7 Ask each group of three to prepare their part of the story in English. Let each group try it out on you. Let them try it out on their neighbouring group. Tell them to try to link their sentences because they will have to try to relate the parts of the story to each other.

8 Ask each group of children to tell the story illustrated by their picture so that the whole story is told.

9 Help each group to write one or two sentences in English under their picture.

FOLLOW-UP 1

Give each child a copy of the story for them to put into their books and illustrate.

FOLLOW-UP 2

This story makes an amusing and simple end-of-term play for parents. You can divide it into nine scenes and change the actors each time. You can make the characters recognizable if they always carry or wear the same thing, for example, the prince can wear a crown and carry a sword, which are handed over to the next prince for the next scene.

3.10 Goldilocks

Once upon a time there were three bears: a big Father bear, a middle-sized Mother bear, and a little Baby bear. The bears lived in a house in the middle of a wood.

One morning they made porridge for breakfast. Father bear poured the hot porridge into three bowls: a small bowl for Baby bear, a middle-sized bowl for Mother bear, and a big bowl for himself. But the porridge was too hot and the bears couldn't eat it. So they went for a walk in the woods while the porridge was cooling.

Just then a little girl called Goldilocks went into the bears' house. Goldilocks saw the three bowls of porridge. She tasted the porridge in the big bowl but that was too hot. She tasted the porridge in the middle-sized bowl and that was too cold. But when Goldilocks tasted the porridge in the little bowl it was just right, and she ate it all up.

Then Goldilocks saw three comfortable chairs. She sat on the big chair but that was too high. She sat on the middle-sized chair but that was too low. She sat on the little chair and that was just right but it broke into a hundred pieces!

Next Goldilocks walked into the bedroom. She saw three beds in a row. She lay down on the big bed, but that was too hard. She lay down on the middle-sized bed, but that was too soft. She lay down on the little bed, and it was just right. Goldilocks fell fast asleep.

When the three bears came home to have breakfast Father bear said: 'Someone has been eating my porridge!'
Mother bear said: 'Someone has been eating my porridge!'

And Baby bear said: 'Someone has been eating my porridge and has eaten it all up!'

Then the three bears saw their chairs. Father bear said: 'Someone has been sitting in my chair!' Mother bear said: 'Someone has been sitting in my chair!' And Baby bear said: 'Someone has been sitting in my chair and it's all broken!'

When the three bears went upstairs and saw their beds, Father bear said: 'Someone has been sleeping in my bed!' Mother bear said: 'Someone has been sleeping in my bed!' And Baby bear said: 'Someone has been sleeping in my bed, and she's still there!'

The bears' voices woke up Goldilocks. She jumped out of bed and ran down the stairs and out of the front door as fast as she could. And Goldilocks never went back to the three bears' house again!

Goldilocks: lesson plan

These activities show that with a careful approach, even beginners can make sense of authentic English. The activities can span several lessons. You need not use them all—choose those most suitable for your children.

LEVEL	**Elementary**
AGE	**6 to 11**
TIME	**100 minutes over several lessons**
LANGUAGE	**Learning new vocabulary; learning to scan texts for meaning well beyond the children's productive capability**
MATERIALS	Card and reusable adhesive such as Blu-tak. It would be enriching for the children, but not essential, if you could get hold of an English-language book of *Goldilocks*.
PREPARATION	1 Make four sets of twelve picture cards (sheet 1, page 116: left-hand side) and twelve word cards (sheet 2, page 117: left-hand side only). Each card should be about 8 cm by 15 cm. You could build the making of them, by the children, into the lesson if you wish.
	2 Make a large, class-sized poster of key sentences in the story with ten words missing (see sheet 3, page 118). Represent each of these missing words with envelopes glued to the poster so that the word cards can then be put in them. The envelopes should be cut in half lengthways so that the word on the card can be

big bear	middle-sized bear	little bear
big bowl	middle-sized bowl	little bowl
big chair	middle-sized chair	little chair

big bed	middle-sized bed

little bed

baby

mother

middle-sized

bowl

bear

porridge

three

wood

big

house

Once upon a time there were ☐ bears:
a big Father ☐ a ☐ Mother
bear and a ☐ bear
The bears lived in a ☐ in the
middle of the ☐ .
One morning they made porridge for
breakfast. Father bear poured the hot
☐ into the three bowls: a small ☐
for Baby bear, a middle-sized bowl for
☐ bear and a ☐ bowl for himself.

seen. It is best to mount the poster on a large piece of card so that it will survive group work.

3 Prepare four sets of ten word cards based on those on the right-hand side of sheet 2. These words are the same as the missing ones on the poster.

4 Write out ten key sentences from the story which tell the gist. Photocopy four sets and cut them into strips of one sentence each.

IN CLASS

1 Tell the story using the twelve picture cards you have made (sheet 1, page 116). Also mime and draw to help the children to understand the story.
As you show the picture cards arrange them on the board with Blu-tack, grouping them to help to teach the words. Write the word for each picture on the board next to it.

2 The children copy the pictures and the words into their folders or exercise books.

3 Tell the story again.

4 Then divide the class into two groups. Each group divides into two groups. The first group play Pelmanism (see 2.10, page 31) with the word cards and picture cards from the story (the same cards as you used on the board). The other group watch and then take their turn. In this way the children learn the word and the written form of it. They also become familiar with the adjectives *big*, *middle-sized*, and *little*.

5 Display the poster of sentences from the Goldilocks story with ten missing words (see Preparation, Steps 2 and 3).

6 Put the children into four equal groups. Give each group an identical set of ten word cards.

7 Read out the sentences, including the words which are missing. Someone from each group runs up to put the missing words on the poster in the right envelopes.

8 Groupwork. Give out the ten sentence strips (see Preparation, Step 4). The children put them into the correct sequence on their tables. They then take it in turns to read any sentence aloud and ask another child to say which one they read. Then they take it in turns to read the whole text.

9 Stick three of the picture cards you made in Preparation, Step 1, illustrating key parts of the story, on to the board or wall.

10 The children stick their sentence strips on to the board or wall under the three key pictures. They only have to search for the key words in each sentence. This 'trains' them to look for key words to decipher difficult texts.

FOLLOW-UP

1 The whole class invent another story based on the same general idea, i.e. somebody goes out of a house and somebody else comes into it. The children take words they have learnt and ask for a few more. They invent the story orally and become familiar with it in this form through retelling.

2 They draw pictures in their folders.

3 Help them to write key sentences from the story. You can keep the sentence patterns and the structures within a very simple range.

Acknowledgements

These activities are based on a set of lesson plans devised by Armida Scarpa.

COMMENTS

Armida Scarpa believes that stories, even in authentic English, can be used from the very beginning. She uses an authentic text of Goldilocks with her class of seven-year-olds who are in their second year at school, still learning to read in Italian, and have English three times a week. She doesn't expect the children to learn these 'advanced' tenses and sentence structures. But she does want to show them that they can make sense of them. She only asks them to really learn the vocabulary. This approach to giving children an experience of authentic English allows you to use almost any story if the children like it and if you approach it carefully.

Children are used to living in a world in which they do not understand a lot of things. To a certain extent they take what we select for them, but they are also aware of all the other information around them. If we deprive children of every experience except those we want them to master, then we rob them of this natural growth.

Pre-intermediate

3.11 The bottom of the sea

It is the year 2010. King Triton lives at the bottom of the sea, in an ivory tower, among weeds and little stones. The sea is very dirty and King Triton and all the fish are very sick and sad.

'Oh, dear. Oh, dear. What can we do?' says one little fish.

'Don't worry,' the king says, 'The fish can clean the water with their fins and the trash cans can eat all the trash.'

So the multi-coloured fish, the sea horses, the eels, the sharks, the dolphins, the starfish, and the crabs clean and clean and clean the sea. The trash cans eat all the trash: all the paper, plastic bags, and plastic bottles, the old tins, and shoes.

Finally, after twenty-five days, they finish the work. The water is clean and transparent, the seaweed is green, and the coral reefs are pink.

King Triton and the fish are not sick now. King Triton invites all the fish to a party at 6:30 p.m. in the whale's mouth.

An eel plays the keyboard, the sea horses play the violins, and the dolphins play the trumpets. Sebastian, the little crab, conducts the orchestra. They all live happily ever after.

Acknowledgements

Adapted from a story written by children (5th class, aged 10, three years of English, 1993/4) at Scuola Elementare Arcobaleno, Cailungo, Republic of San Marino. It was submitted for the '21st Century Fairy Tale: *JET* Story Competition'.

The bottom of the sea: lesson plan

The children listen to a story written by children aged ten after three years of English in San Marino, understand it, and recognize the words they have been introduced to.

LEVEL	**Elementary**
AGE	**8 to 12**
TIME	**35 minutes**
LANGUAGE	**Developing the ability to listen to a story containing a lot of new words but still being able to follow the gist of it**
MATERIALS	Have a large piece of paper and a set of large felt-tip pens ready. Make sure you have somewhere to display the paper.
PREPARATION	1 The objects are not too difficult to draw but you might feel more confident if you practise beforehand. See the examples on page 122 and Chapter 7, page 207 for tips.

2 Write ten sentences from the story, in the wrong order, on another large sheet of paper.

 L The fish clean the sea.
 N The fish are not sick.
 E After 25 days the water is clean.
 X The sea is dirty.

L The trash cans eat the trash.
C All the fish are sick.
T They have a party.
E King Triton lives in a castle.
E 'Don't worry!' the king says.

Photocopiable © Oxford University Press

IN CLASS

1 Write the following words on the board: *bottom, sea, tower, weeds, stones, fish, trash, can, sea horse, eel, shark, dolphin, starfish, crab, plastic bottle, tin, whale.*

2 Draw a wavy line near the top of the large piece of paper and say *This is the sea.* Then draw a hilly line at the bottom and say *This is the bottom of the sea.*

3 Teach the phrase *Please draw a . . ..* Write it on the board and invite the children to tell you which objects from the list to draw. Keep on saying their English names as you draw them. Ask the class to repeat each word in chorus, and for some of the children to repeat it for you. Pretend to admire your drawing and praise it! *It's a lovely tower, isn't it?* Ask questions about the things you draw, for example, *Have you seen a shark?*

4 Play a game of 'describe and identify'.
You: *It's a horse but it lives in the sea.*
Children: *It's a sea-horse.*

5 Tell the story, miming sadness and sweeping the sea clean.

6 Tell the children the story was written by a class of children in San Marino for a story competition (*JET* 1994). Ask them if they like the story.

7 Ask them to choose and write down one word from the board that they like, and one word they don't like. Tell them that you will tell the story again and this time they must jump up and sit down every time they hear either of their words. Tell the story and let them jump up and sit down.

8 Tell them you will repeat the same activity, but this time they must watch to see which words their neighbour has chosen.

9 They discuss with their neighbours which words they think each one has chosen, and which they think is the word they like and which is the word they don't like.

10 Show the ten muddled sentences. Tell the children to imagine what sequence they should be in to tell the story and to copy the initial capital letters. If they write these letters out in the correct sequence they will get the word 'EXCELLENT'. If they can do this, you can say that their work is excellent!

FOLLOW-UP 1

The children can make their own picture of the sea and its creatures in their books; and on the opposite page write out the ten sentences which summarize the story in the correct sequence.

FOLLOW-UP 2

This story can obviously be related to the topic of pollution.

FOLLOW-UP 3

The story can be rewritten by the children and set in a different context.

COMMENTS

It is not important for the children to retain all the words for the sea creatures.

Please note that 'trash' and 'trash can' are the American English equivalents of the British English 'rubbish' and 'dustbin'. You can choose according to which variety of English you teach.

Pre-intermediate

3.12 Strange animal

Sipo was an African boy. He lived in a village with his family: his

his parents, brothers, sisters, and auntie. They were all very nice to him—except his auntie.

Every day his auntie shouted at him, 'Do this! Do that!' She shouted so much that she frightened the birds!

Sipo didn't like his auntie. Sometimes he thought, 'I'll get some medicine and I'll put it into her food to make her quiet.' But he didn't do it.

One day his auntie shouted, 'You are a lazy boy! You are always playing your drum! You never work! You must go to the trees by the cliffs. There is a lot of fruit there.'

Sipo didn't want to go to the trees by the cliffs. He was frightened. His friend said, 'There is a strange animal there. It lives in the caves.'

'Go! Go! Go!' said his auntie. So he took a bag and his drum and he went.

He walked and he walked and he walked. It was a long way to the cliffs. At last he arrived. The trees were full of fruit. His auntie was right. Sipo began to pick the fruit. Suddenly he heard a noise! He turned and there was a huge, strange animal! His friend was right! Sipo was very frightened. He took his drum and he began to beat it. He played and played his drum!

The strange animal stopped. He was surprised! He began to dance! Sipo played and played and the strange animal danced and danced! When Sipo was tired and stopped playing, the animal walked towards him. So he played again! Sipo played all day; he played all morning and he played all afternoon. At last it was night time, it was dark. Suddenly, the monster stopped dancing and it turned and it walked into the dark bushes.

Sipo ran back home. He arrived in the village and his auntie shouted, 'You lazy boy! Where is the fruit?' But Sipo had no fruit. His bag was on the ground by the trees by the cliffs. So his auntie beat him with a stick. 'You lazy boy. You played your drum, I know. It's true, isn't it?'
'Yes, auntie. But there was a strange animal!'
'You lazy boy!' And she beat him again.

Sipo told his father, 'Father it is true. There was a strange animal there. I saw it. I played my drum and it danced. I couldn't pick the fruit.'
'Tomorrow I will come with you, my son.'

The next morning, Sipo and his father and his mother and his auntie all walked to the cliffs. There were the trees full of fruit. 'Give me your drum!' shouted his auntie and she took it and tied it high in a tree.
'Auntie! Auntie! The strange animal will come!'
'Shut up, you lazy boy, and pick some fruit!'

Suddenly the strange animal came. It went to Sipo's father and ate him and then to Sipo's mother and ate her. Sipo's auntie ran away and the strange animal ran after her and ate her too. Sipo climbed the tree and got his drum.

Then Sipo played his drum! And the strange animal began to dance! Sipo began to play faster and faster! The strange animal began to dance faster and faster! Sipo played faster and the strange animal danced faster!

Suddenly, the strange animal began to be sick . . . and suddenly Sipo's father and then his mother came out of the strange animal's mouth! Sipo played more slowly. He was very happy! 'Play more quickly!' shouted his father. 'Your auntie is still inside him!'
'Oh, father! I don't want to!' said Sipo.
'Play faster!'

Sipo played faster and faster and the strange animal danced faster and faster. Suddenly, Sipo's auntie came out of the strange animal's mouth! At last evening came and the strange animal went into the dark bushes. Sipo stopped playing and he and his mother and father and his auntie walked home. His auntie was very quiet.

Sipo's auntie never shouted again. And sometimes she said, 'Sipo's a good boy!'

Acknowledgements

Adapted from *Children of Wax: African Folk Tales* by Alexander McCall Smith, published by Canongate Books Ltd., 1994 (see Further Reading).

Strange animal: lesson plan

Here is another way of designing a lesson plan which can be applied to most stories. In this case it is applied to 'Strange animal', a powerful African story which shows we all share the same family problems and the same fear of the unknown.

LEVEL	Pre-intermediate
AGE	10 to 14
TIME	70 minutes
LANGUAGE	**Introducing the past tense in its written form (and future tense briefly); fluency in all four skills; new vocabulary**
MATERIALS	Bring in some fruit and a drum if you can—or at least an old tin; a bag, preferably an old leather or cloth bag.
PREPARATION	1 Be ready to draw the simple pictures on the board or on a large sheet of paper (see In Class, Step 2).

2 Make word flash cards for the key words:
Africa   boy   village   family   shout   trees by the
cliff   fruit   dark bushes   drum   dance

3 Make sentence strips of past tense forms if you want the
children to become consciously familiar with them (see Step 12).

4 Make an A4 sheet of jumbled sentences based on those given
in Step 12 below.

IN CLASS

Before the story

1 Begin by drumming (even if you are not an experienced
drummer!). If you are using a box or a tin you can introduce the
word for drum by saying *This isn't a box, it's a drum!*

2 Draw simple pictures on the board of key items of vocabulary
from the story, in the order in which they occur in the story.
Don't write the words. In 'Strange animal' the words might be:

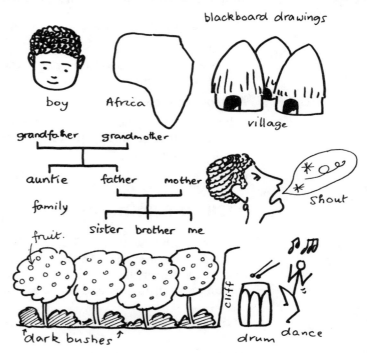

blackboard drawings

Make a gesture of some distinctive kind for each word. Be
consistent in using this gesture during this stage.

Say the words rapidly, each time making the gesture you have
chosen for them and pointing at the pictures.

Note: instead of pictures you might have a real drum, or a
basket of fruit to show that various fruits make fruit!

3 Give out word cards to a number of children. Ask them to come to the board and stick them next to their picture, or to write the word there instead.

4 Then make the gesture you have associated with the word but don't say the word. Look at the children and expect them to give you the word. Keep this up at a fast pace to raise the excitement.

5 Show the word cards to the class at the same time and get the children to say the word.

6 Mouth the words silently and see if the children can guess the word you are mouthing.

7 Tell the children to close their eyes and to call out the words they remember.

During the story

8 As you tell the story use a lot of mime and use the same gestures for key words you showed the children in Step 2. Use the drum, the bag, and the fruit if you have them. I often get the children to drum on the floor if they are sitting on the floor or on a table if they are sitting at tables.

9 Tell the children to close their eyes. Tell the story a second time. Ask the children what they saw, for example:
Is Sipo a big boy or a small boy? What is he like? How is he dressed? What is the countryside like? What is the house like?

After the story

Make sure that everyone has understood the story and that it has 'sunk in'.

10 Using your pictures, help the children, as a class, to retell the story.

11 Say the sentences on page 128. Put the sentence strips on the board and ask all the children to mime them. If they can do this while standing in a big, clear space it would be better—if not, then in their places.

12 Hand out the A4 sheet of jumbled sentences. Ask the children to number them in the correct order. Now give each child one sentence and ask them to read out the sentences in the correct order (each child reads their own sentence). Alternatively, cut the sentences into separate strips and then ask the children to arrange them in the correct sequence and to stick them in their books.

13 Ask individual children to mime any sentence. Other children guess which sentence is being mimed.

14 Take down the sentence strips and give one to some children. Ask them to come to the front of the class and to mime so that the other children can guess which sentence strip they have.

15 Pairwork: children take it in turns to mime a sentence and their partner guesses which one it is.

Every day his auntie shouted at him.
He began to pick the fruit.
There was a huge, strange animal.
He played and played his drum.
The strange animal danced and danced and danced.
Sipo went home.
Sipo and his parents and auntie went to the cliffs.
She tied the drum in a tree.
Sipo's auntie ran away.
Sipo climbed a tree and got his drum.
The animal danced faster and faster.
Suddenly the strange animal was sick.
His father and his mother came out of the animal's mouth.
Sipo played more slowly.
Sipo played faster.
Suddenly Sipo's auntie came out of the animal's mouth.
The strange animal went into the bushes.

Photocopiable © Oxford University Press

16 Retell the story, making mistakes, for example:
Sipo was a Chinese girl.
His uncle shouted at him.
The children correct you.

17 Ask the class to retell the story.

18 Pairwork. Ask each child to take it in turns to try to retell the story. They should help each other. You cannot hope to monitor all the children while they do this.

FOLLOW-UP 1   Topic work: relate this story to its African background (it comes from Zimbabwe) and do topic work on Africa: geography, history, culture, etc.

FOLLOW-UP 2   Dramatize the story, following on from the miming. See 2.94, 'Guidelines for dramatizing stories'.

FOLLOW-UP 3   The children make a long mural picture strip to illustrate the sentences.

COMMENTS

Not all the steps need to be done in the same lesson, or at all! Choose those which are most appropriate for your children.

Acknowledgements

My ideas in this lesson plan are closely modelled on those of Günther Gerngross.

3.13 Elidor

Once upon a time there was a boy in Wales, called Elidor. He didn't like school and he didn't work very hard. When he learnt one thing, he forgot another. The teacher was angry and beat him with a stick, but he learnt nothing.

One day Elidor was so unhappy that he ran away! Elidor ran down to the river. He knew the river very well. He knew all the best places to hide. Elidor hid by the bank of the river. Nobody could find him there.

He thought, 'I'll stay here until teatime. They will look for me. They will be very worried and they will be sorry, really sorry, because they were so unkind to me.'

The evening came and it began to grow dark. Elidor stayed by the bank above the river. 'I won't go home tonight. I'll stay here all night. They will be really worried.'

Elidor stayed all night and all the next day. Then he decided to stay the next night as well and all the next day! He stayed there for two days and nights. During the third evening two little men came to him. They were very small, only the height of Elidor's knee!

'What are you doing here?' they asked him.
Elidor told them how unhappy he was because the teachers beat him.
'Oh, in our land children are always happy and nobody beats them. Why don't you come with us?'

So Elidor agreed to go with them. The two little men walked along the bank of the river until they came to a large hole. They walked into the hole and Elidor followed them; he crawled on his hands and knees. Elidor crawled for a long way. At last he saw some light ahead of him and then he came out into a new land of fields and trees and hills. There were corn-fields and farmers were cutting the corn. The farmers were the same size as the two little men who were with Elidor. The farmers' horses were as big as dogs. The two little men took Elidor to the king's palace. The king was very kind, 'Of course you can stay in my land. And you can play with my son, the prince.'

Elidor played with the prince; they played with a golden ball.

At last Elidor wanted to go home to see his mother. 'Of course you can go, Elidor!' said the king, 'You can come and go as you wish.'

So Elidor went across the fields and through the hole, to the river and then home to his mother. She was very pleased to see him.

After some time Elidor went back again to the land of the small people to play with the prince. He often went to the land of the little people.

Elidor told his mother about that world and all the gold that was there.
'Oh, Elidor, you know we are very poor. Bring some gold back with you next time.' Elidor didn't want to take any gold from the little people but he wanted to help his mother.

The next time he played with the prince he took the golden ball and ran across the fields. The two little men ran after him, 'Elidor, come back. Come back! Don't take the golden ball!'

Elidor ran across the fields, through the hole, to the river and back home. The two little men ran after him. Elidor opened his mother's door and he fell into the kitchen. He dropped the ball and the two little men shouted 'Elidor!'. They took the ball and then ran away and down to the river.

Elidor ran after them but he could not catch them. He went to the river but he could not find the hole! He looked and he looked for hours but he could not find it anywhere.
Elidor came the next day and the next but he could not find the hole. He never found it again.

Many years later, when Elidor was an old man, people sometimes asked him about the land of the little people. Tears came to his eyes when he remembered what he had done and what he had lost.

Acknowledgements

This story is based on one written by Gerald of Wales in 1191.

Elidor: lesson plan 1

LEVEL	**Pre-intermediate**
AGE	**9 to 14**
TIME	**40 minutes**
LANGUAGE	**Skills: listening fluency and speaking fluency through simple retelling; summarizing and sequencing; past tense; new vocabulary**
MATERIALS	A big piece of paper for the map; a small piece of paper (about A5) for each child; scissors to cut out their pictures; glue or pins to stick the pictures on to the big piece of paper; and a big, blue felt-tip pen for the child who draws the river.
PREPARATION	**1** Practise telling the story.

2 Make word cards with the following words written on them:
a school   a boy   a big stick   a river   the moon
two little men   a large hole (tunnel)
a tunnel through a hill   fields of corn
a little man on a little horse   trees   a palace   a king
a prince   a ball   a house

The words must be large enough to read from a distance.

3 Put up the big piece of paper on the wall.

IN CLASS

1 Tell the children that you will tell them a story but that you need them to draw some pictures for it before you begin. Tell them that they are going to make a map of the story together.

2 Give each child a word card and a piece of paper to draw on. Make sure that everyone knows what each word means. They should draw what is on their card. Begin with the words which will take longer to draw, for example, the school. If you have more than sixteen children, two children might work on the same picture, and some children can draw extra trees so that each child has something to draw.

Tell them their picture must only show the object you have given them without any background. It must be clearly drawn and be about as big as their hand so that other children can see it when it is put on the map. The child doing the river should draw it directly on the big piece of paper near the bottom, with the big, blue felt-tip pen.

If they find the drawing very difficult, you can give them one of my pictures to copy.

Have the scissors ready for the children to cut out the shape of
their picture.

During this step in the activity repeat the words very often and
ask the class to repeat them with you.

3 Display the pictures on the wall or on tables (not on the map
yet). Ask the children to look at the pictures and to predict what
they can about the story. They can try to predict the sequence in
which the pictures will be referred to. You might ask them to
stand in the sequence they predict, in a big circle, holding their
pictures. They will need the connecting word then.

4 Collect the word cards and then give them out to different
children.

5 Tell the story. As the children hear the word on their word
card they should hold it up and then go to the right picture, take
it down, and give it to you.

Stick the picture on the map. Keep the house and school on one
side, the hole and tunnel in the middle, and the fields and palace
on the other side. Don't stick down the boy and the two little
men. Everything else should be stuck down permanently.

You can hold the pictures of the boy and the two little men and
move them.

Keep the word cards on your table.

6 Ask for volunteers to retell the story, guided by the map and
pictures. Here is an example of a retelling of the story which
pre-intermediate students might manage to approximate:

> There was a boy. His name was Elidor. He was not very
> good at school. His teachers hit him with a stick. One day
> he ran away. He ran to the river and he hid by the bank of

Map of Elidor's journey

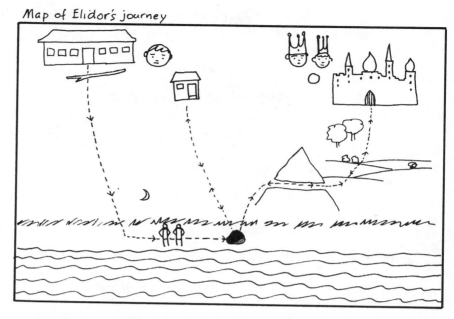

the river. He stayed there for two days and nights. Then two little men came. He followed them. They went into a tunnel and then they came out in a new land. They went to a palace and Elidor met the king. Elidor played with the prince. They played with a golden ball. One day Elidor went home to see his mother. His mother said she wanted some gold. Elidor went to the palace again and he took the golden ball. The two little men ran after Elidor. Elidor got home but he dropped the golden ball. The two little men took the ball. Elidor ran after them but he couldn't find the tunnel. He looked for the tunnel for a long time. When he was old he was very sad because he took [had taken] the golden ball.

FOLLOW-UP 1

Follow this lesson with the second lesson plan.

FOLLOW-UP 2

The children each draw a map and pictures and write the story in their books.

COMMENTS

1 This technique can be used with any story in which there is a journey which the children can represent with a map and in which there are objects and people which can be drawn by the children and placed on the map.

See: 3.7, 'Little Red Riding Hood', 3.4, 'The little Indian boy', 3.12, 'Strange animal', 6.6, 'The boy who cried wolf', 3.14, 'Tom Thumb'.

2 The children encounter a high proportion of language which might be beyond them, but they should manage to get enough of the story to enjoy it. This provides excellent training in listening fluency, strengthening their confidence, and developing their skill

in looking for meaning from any clue (linguistic or non-linguistic).

Elidor: lesson plan 2

'Elidor' is dramatized in this second lesson.

LEVEL   **Pre-intermediate**

AGE   **12 +**

TIME   **80 minutes**

LANGUAGE   **Prepositions; words for feelings; four skills fluency**

PREPARATION   Have ready the map the children made in the previous lesson.

IN CLASS   1 By brief questions focus the children's minds back to the story of Elidor and see if the class can retell the story. As the class reconstruct the story, you can make a flow chart of it as follows:

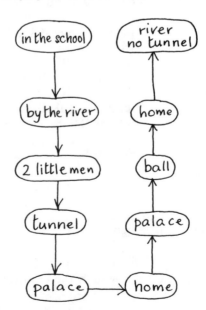

2 Ask the children to write down the three most important moments in the story for them and to compare their sentences with their neighbour's choice.

You might feel they need preparing for this by listing phrases which help them to identify those moments:

in the school   by the river bank   by the river bank with
the two little men   in the tunnel   in the fields   at the
palace   with the prince   at home   taking the ball   at
home and dropping the ball   at the end of the story.

Alternatively, at a higher language level:

In the school when the teachers hit him
By the river bank when he hides
By the river bank when the two little men come
At the palace with the king
At the palace when he takes the ball
At the end of the story when he is an old man.

3 Have a general class discussion about these important
moments but avoid any feeling of there being three 'correct'
moments to have chosen.

Ask how the characters in the story felt at these various
moments. Write the words on the board above and below
the flow chart.

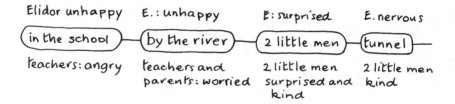

Elidor unhappy   E.: unhappy   E: surprised   E. nervous
(in the school)—(by the river)—(2 little men)—(tunnel)—
teachers: angry   teachers and   2 little men   2 little men
                      parents: worried   surprised and   kind
                                          kind

Teach the children the words they do not know by mime
and facial expression. Ask the children to give you the word
in their mother tongue to confirm that they have understood
your mime!

Test understanding by miming and then by asking the
children how you feel.

Let children take over your role. Then ask the children to
work in pairs, miming for each other, until the words are
fairly well grasped.

4 Divide the class into eight groups (the story divides into
eight parts). Give each group a scene to act. They must do
their best to convey the feelings of the participants. You
might even introduce each scene with the words for the
feelings which are going to be expressed.

You will need a different number of children in each group.
Below are the minimum number of characters in each
scene. More children can easily be given extra parts in any
of the scenes (see 2.94, Guidelines on dramatizing stories,
page 70). Elidor should have a hat or scarf so that he can be
identified from scene to scene as different children play his
part.

Scene 1: Elidor, teacher
Scene 2: Elidor
Scene 3: Elidor, two little men
Scene 4: Elidor, two little men, king, prince
Scene 5: Elidor, king/mother
Scene 6: Elidor, mother
Scene 7: Elidor, prince, two little men, mother
Scene 8: Elidor.

5 The groups take it in turns to dramatize their scenes and so build up the whole story.

FOLLOW-UP 1

Follow this lesson with the third lesson.

FOLLOW-UP 2

Each group can draw and write their scene on a large poster. All the posters can then be displayed in the room as a long frieze.

Elidor: lesson plan 3

LEVEL

Pre-intermediate

AGE

12 to 14

TIME

40 minutes

LANGUAGE

Words for feeling; writing the story

MATERIALS

A narrow strip of paper for each child (see Preparation, step 2); A2 paper; glue to stick down the strips; A3 paper for the sentences.

PREPARATION

1 You must feel confident you can show the children what an abstract picture story is—better try it out yourself before the lesson!

2 Make a narrow strip of paper for each child, e.g. by cutting A4 paper lengthwise into two.

IN CLASS

1 Introduce the children to the idea of 'abstract picture stories' by drawing these three lines on the board. Ask which line is happy, nervous, or angry.

2 List all the words for feelings the children know (see 'Elidor': second lesson plan). Take one of these words for feelings but this time use shapes and other abstract elements like tone, texture, and colour as well. Here is an example:

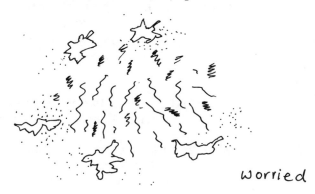

worried

Ask the children which word you have tried to represent.

3 Invite the children to come to the board and represent one of the words of feeling with an abstract line or shape. Ask the other children to guess which he or she has tried to represent. Agree with the children that it is difficult to make a drawing which everybody agrees on. There is no absolute right or wrong; some shapes and lines most people can agree on but others are more personal.

4 Tell the children you are going to ask them to make an abstract picture story of 'Elidor'. Demonstrate how to make an expressive picture representation of the first part of the story. Write in the words for feelings next to your abstract representation of them, and write a number under each part and write a sentence for each number below. Here is my example, but remember, there is no right or wrong in this and you might do it quite differently!

Here are the sentences for the numbers:

    1 *The teacher was angry.*
    2 *He beat Elidor with a stick.*
    3 *Elidor was very unhappy.*

5 Make up groups of eight children. Each group is responsible for making one abstract picture story. Each child within the group makes one or two of the eight parts to the story. They should draw their part of the abstract picture story on their strip of paper, horizontally. They should write their sentences on another piece of paper. The children must stick down their abstract picture strip in the correct sequence on a large piece of paper (A2) and their sentences on another piece of paper (A3).

6 Display the abstract picture stories. See if children from the different groups can interpret the other groups' abstract picture stories.

FOLLOW-UP 1   The children might like to illustrate the words for feeling in two ways: (1) abstract lines (2) facial expressions.

FOLLOW-UP 2   A different kind of activity would be to ask individual children to sit in front of the class and be interviewed by the class as if they were one of the characters: 'How did you feel when . . .', etc.

3.14 Tom Thumb

1 A man and a woman live in a cottage in a wood. They are unhappy.
'We've got a nice cottage,' says the wife.
'And we've got a nice garden,' says the husband.
'But we haven't got any children,' says the wife.
'And we want a little child,' says the husband.

2 Merlin the Magician hears the man and the woman and he gives them a little child. It is a very little child! It is five centimetres tall!
'What's his name?' they ask Merlin.
'Tom Thumb,' he says.

3 One day Tom Thumb is walking in a field. Suddenly a big black raven sees him. The raven flies down and picks up Tom. The raven flies over the fields and the farms and over hills and towns. 'Hey! You! Put me down!' Tom Thumb shouts.
Then the raven flies over the sea and drops Tom into the waves! A big fish swallows Tom. Tom goes into the stomach of the fish.

4 A fisherman catches the fish and takes it to the land. The king's cook buys the fish, takes it to the palace, and cuts it open. There is Tom!
The cook goes to King Arthur. 'King Arthur! Look! There's a very small young man in this fish!'
All the knights and the ladies laugh and laugh and laugh!
'Ho! Ho! Ho! Ho! Ho! Ho! Ho! Ho! Ho! Ho!'
King Arthur says, 'Stay here! Stay with us!'

5 One day King Arthur says, 'Are your parents big or small?'
Tom says, 'They are big—but they are poor!'
'They are poor?' says King Arthur, 'You must take them some
money! Come into my treasury!'
Tom takes a little gold coin.

6 Tom puts the coin on his back and he walks home to his parents.
His mother and father are very happy!
'Hello, Tom!'
'Hello, Mum! Hello, Dad! I live with King Arthur. Here's some
money.
But I must go now.'
'Oh dear!' says Tom's mum, 'But thank you for the money!'

7 Tom walks to King Arthur's palace. In the night Tom sleeps
in a snail shell. In the morning he catches a big butterfly and
rides on her back. The butterfly flies over the fields and over the
woods and, at last, to the palace. The knights see the butterfly
and see Tom and they chase him. At last he falls off the butterfly
into a watering can. He can't swim!
'Help! Help!'
A knight lifts Tom out of the water.

8 One day a large spider attacks Tom. Tom fights with his
sword but the spider bites him! Tom dies!
'I'm dead!'

King Arthur and all the knights and ladies are very sad. They
cry and they cry.
'Boohoo! Boohoo! Boohoo!'
They make a gravestone for Tom. They write on the gravestone:

Here lies Tom Thumb
King Arthur's knight
A spider gave him
A cruel bite!

Tom Thumb: lesson plan

The children predict a story-line from muddled pictures and then
act the story out scene by scene.

LEVEL	**Pre-intermediate**
AGE	**9 to 11**
TIME	**70 minutes**
LANGUAGE	**Listening and speaking fluency; prepositions**

PREPARATION

1 Photocopy eight sets of the eight pictures for the story (see page 140). Cut them up.

IN CLASS

1 Divide the children into eight groups. Give each group a complete set of eight pictures, cut up. Ask the groups to put the pictures into the sequence they think the story will follow.

2 Ask which sequence the groups have put their pictures in (this will entail describing the pictures).

Examples

In the first one there are two people and a cottage in a wood.
In the second one there is a man in a tall black hat.

Do not confirm or reject any ideas at this stage, but encourage differences of opinion.

3 Tell the story.

4 Discuss which order the pictures should be in.

5 Tell the children they are going to dramatize the story and there will be nine scenes. In each scene there will be a different number of people. Go through the story, indicating each of the eight scenes (as shown in the text on page 138–9). Ask the children how many children should be in each scene. The basic numbers are:

Scene 1: man and wife
Scene 2: Merlin, Tom Thumb, man, and wife
Scene 3: raven, Tom Thumb
Scene 4: fisherman, fish, cook, Tom Thumb, king, knights, ladies
Scene 5: king, Tom Thumb
Scene 6: Tom Thumb, man, and wife
Scene 7: butterfly, Tom Thumb, two or three knights
Scene 8: spider, Tom Thumb, king, knights, ladies.

Note that the raven, the fish, the butterfly, and the spider can all be made out of several children. Additional children can also be inanimate objects, for example, trees making a wood.

This story is written for dramatizing with a narrator. See also 2.94, 'Guidelines for dramatizing stories', on page 70.

6 Act out the play with each group doing its scene. One way of dealing with the tiny size of Tom Thumb is to use a small doll or even a symbol for him like an eraser carried on a child's hand. An alternative is for the child playing Tom Thumb to crouch all the time.

7 Tell the class that they will act the story again, but this time you want one of the inanimate objects in each scene to say something which can be echoed and modified by the rest of the class, for example, in the first scene:

The cottage door: *How sad! They've got a cottage but they haven't got a baby.*

Class, inventing alternative sentiments:
How sad! They've got a garden but they haven't got a baby.
How sad! They've got a car but they haven't got a baby.
How sad! They've got a television but they haven't got a baby.

You might have to help! List all the echoes on the board and then the whole class can echo-chorus them.

COMMENTS

The main purpose in dramatization is to help the children not merely to understand the language but to feel that they own it. Dramatization can lead to a performance to an audience outside the class, but that is not the purpose behind the ideas given here.

FOLLOW-UP

Write and perform more adventures of Tom Thumb. It is unlikely to move people as 'Elidor' does, so it doesn't matter if the children make fun of it!

Acknowledgments

I got the idea of chorusing the comments of inanimate objects from *Teaching Myself* by Bernard Dufeu (see Further Reading).

3.15 Nessy

Mr and Mrs Poppleton and their son Paul were on holiday in Scotland. Paul wanted to go to Loch Ness. He wanted to see the Loch Ness Monster.

Paul walked along the side of the Loch. The water of the Loch was very flat. There was no monster.

Suddenly Paul saw a large green rock. It was very round and smooth. It began to move. Then it opened! It was an egg! An enormous egg!

A small monster was sitting in the egg. The little monster saw Paul and thought, 'That's my daddy!'

Paul ran to his parents. They were sitting in the car. They saw the little monster coming.
'Quick! Get in the car!' they said, and they drove away.

The little monster tried to follow the car. He saw his daddy in the car—Paul!

At last Mr Poppleton stopped the car. They waited for the little monster and then Paul picked it up and got back in the car. They drove home.

Paul kept the little monster in his bedroom. He called her Nessy. Nessy grew bigger. She was very strong. Paul could ride on her back. Nessy could jump up and down.

Nessy could count. Paul held up three fingers and Nessy hit her tail on the floor three times.

But Nessy grew bigger and bigger and bigger. And she became hungrier and hungrier and hungrier. One day Nessy came downstairs for breakfast but then she could not go upstairs again.

Mr Poppleton put his car in the street. Nessy lived in the garage.

Nessy was very hungry. One night she got out of the garage and went to a chocolate factory and ate all the chocolate. The police came and then everybody in the town knew: the Poppleton family had a monster!

Mr and Mrs Poppleton and Paul decided to take Nessy back to Scotland. They got a big lorry and put Nessy on it and then drove all the way to Loch Ness. Nessy's mum was there! Nessy and her mum played by the Loch, then they swam in the water, and then they dived. Paul and his mum waited by the side of the Loch. The water became flat. Nessy and her mum did not come back.

Paul said, 'Mum, let's come back in exactly one year. Perhaps Nessy will come to see us.'

Acknowledgements

Adapted from *Nessy* by Andrew Wright (see Further Reading)

Nessy: lesson plan

LEVEL	**Pre-intermediate**
AGE	**8 to 12**
TIME	**80 minutes**
LANGUAGE	**Passive exposure to past tenses; topic work on monsters; adjectives; *can* for ability**
MATERIALS	Large strips of paper for the children to write sentences on (Step 12); illustrations and sentence cards as in the Preparation.
PREPARATION	**1** Make sure the board is clean and ready for you to divide into half (Step 1). **2** Photocopy the Nessy illustrations (page 145) for the children or be ready to draw them on the board as you tell the story.

3 Prepare two texts, each with different gaps (Step 9).

4 Prepare a simple comprehension worksheet (Step 10), for example:

> gap filling: *The Poppleton family were on holiday in* _____.
>
> sentence sequencing: *The police came. Nessy could count.*
> true/false: *Nessy bit Mr Poppleton.*

IN CLASS

1 Introduce the topic of monsters, and help the children to make statements about the topic making use of all the language they have at their command. Supply them with the key words they need.

2 Divide the board in half with a vertical line. Ask for two children to come to the board in order to draw, each on one half of the board.

The children draw two contrasting pictures on the board, according to the instructions of the teacher and the other children in the class. For example, a monster with a long nose, little eyes, a big mouth, etc., contrasted with a monster which has a short nose, big eyes, and a little mouth. This activity allows the children to experience and understand the language used in relationship to pictures which they can see.
(See also *Young Learners* in this series, page 123: 'Twin plasticine monsters'.)

3 Lead a discussion of the physical characteristics of monsters: *big, strong,* etc.

4 Lead a discussion of the possible other characteristics of monsters, for example, *good, nice, friendly, angry, dangerous, gentle,* etc.

5 Lead a discussion of things monsters can do, for example,

A monster can hurt you
It can carry you
It can eat you.

6 Read or tell the Nessy story, showing pictures, miming actions, etc., and sometimes checking to make sure that the children understand.

7 Ask questions about the story in order to check that the children have understood the gist of it.

8 Pairwork. Each child has a text or a number of different texts from the story with missing words. The words missing are different for each partner in the pair. Together they work out the missing words.

9 Give the children a simple comprehension worksheet. Various types of activity can be used, including:

- gap filling
- sentence sequencing
- true/false sentences.

10 The children try to remember sentences from the story, call them out, and you write them on the board, in any order. The children copy the sentences and/or create more. Help each child to choose one sentence which the child must then copy on to a large strip of paper. These strip sentences are then arranged to produce an attractive poster.

11 Lead a discussion in which the children suggest possible titles for a new story they would like to make up. The new story should be somehow related to the one they have been working on. For example, they might take the same characters and put them into a different setting and situation.

12 Pairwork: the children invent a dialogue from one of the story titles they listed in 11 above. They practise it aloud but do not write it down.

13 In pairs, the children perform their dialogues for each other.

14 As a class (or in pairs or as individuals) the children now select a title and invented dialogue, expand it into a story, and write it down. This can be done in book form and not just into their exercise books. You should of course check the sentences for accuracy. The children might have to make two drafts: first and final.

15 Let the children take the books home to show their families. Perhaps put them into the school library.

Acknowledgements

This lesson plan was devised by Leslie Cohen.

COMMENTS

1 Leslie Cohen uses stories as the basis of all her teaching in the second year. If the story is carefully chosen and then introduced and carefully presented, it is possible for even the weakest children to understand and enjoy it. You can pick and choose from this list of activities and adapt them to the variety of children's levels, needs, topics, and interests. They can also be used with other topics, for example, prehistoric cave people or the environment.

2 Leslie Cohen prefers to postpone the written stage and to take very small steps towards it, which is particularly important for young beginners, especially when they are not familiar with the Roman alphabet.

4 Topics and stories

Why combine topic study with stories?

There is a lot to be said for letting children just enjoy a story without asking them to do very much about it. Already this can be a rich experience for the child: he or she is pleased to hear the story and encouraged to realize that it is within his or her power to understand ten or fifteen minutes of continuous English. And it is the best training possible in listening fluency.

However, sometimes it is also enriching for the child to experience the story as a door to all kinds of other experiences. Stories can provide a linking thread to cross-curricular studies. Through stories and related activities, children can develop their understanding of the world around them and of their own ability to explore that world by hypothesizing, comparing, grouping, sequencing, etc. in subject areas:

- geography: location, climate, physical appearance of countries and using geographical techniques, for example, map making
- history: awareness of time and human development
- sociology: what people give value to and how they behave
- science: habitats of animals, the food they eat, ecology, materials, etc.
- art and crafts: pictures, books, designs
- drama and music: writing and telling stories, miming and acting, finding or making music to accompany stories.

How much time is necessary?

If all you do is look at a map of the world to find out where China is for the 'Ma Liang' story (3.8) you can say you have related topics and stories, and that is five minutes of work! On the other hand, some teachers who make stories central to their teaching of English might make a study of topics related to one story last for six months. (Silvana Aurilia 1994). You can thus choose to spend any amount of time between five minutes and six months on linking topics with a story!

How can the language be linked to the syllabus?

If your language syllabus is based on areas of language which are potentially useful to the child then it follows that much of your work on topics will use areas of language which already form part of your language syllabus. There is no necessary conflict between the two.

The most important thing is that the children experience the language you are teaching them as useful and relevant for dealing with their experience.

A practical approach to lesson planning

1 Draw a topic web based on the story you have chosen. The web below is based on 'Town Mouse and Country Mouse'.

2 Jot down some purposeful activities you might make use of, which are both relevant to the topic, and at the same time give children appropriate practice in using English.

3 Pick out those topics which make use of the sort of language you would like the children to learn.

4 Decide whether to tell or read the story in parts or as a whole. 'Town Mouse and Country Mouse' is so short that it is probably best done as a whole, or at most in two parts.

5 Introduce and practise key vocabulary before the story and then tell or read it.

6 Embark on the topic-related activities. You will probably repeatedly return to the original story as the topic work proceeds.

Town Mouse and Country Mouse

Eva Benkö, who works with children aged ten to twelve in Budapest, Hungary, has provided the majority of activities for 'Town Mouse and Country Mouse'. I am grateful to her for this rich addition to the book. It is worth noting that Hungarian is unlike any other European language (except Finnish in some respects). This makes it particularly challenging for Hungarian children to learn English. In spite of the difficulties for children learning English in Hungary, you will notice that Eva believes that they should meet a wide range of 'natural' English. She is also quite happy for the children to use their mother tongue to discuss ideas which arise from the activities.

I have used 'Town Mouse and Country Mouse' as an example because it is so short and simple and yet offers so much rich, topic-related study. You will probably want to make a selection of the activities offered; each full sequence would take several weeks to do. As with all activities, you must judge which individual activities are suitable for the age, level, and interests of your class.

For more on the linking of topics with stories see Ellis and Brewster 1991: *The Storytelling Handbook for Primary Teachers* (see Further Reading).

4.1 Town Mouse and Country Mouse: story

A Town Mouse visits a Country Mouse.

He says, 'What a nice house!'
But he thinks, 'This house is not a nice house, it's a hole in the ground!'
He says, 'What nice food!'
But he thinks, 'This food is not nice food, it's corn!'

The Country Mouse visits the Town Mouse.

He says, 'What a nice house!'
The Town Mouse says, 'Thank you. Now come and eat. You can have Brie cheese, Gorgonzola cheese, or cottage cheese. You can have sausage, potatoes, beans, carrots, or lettuce. You can have honey, bread, cake . . . '
'What's that noise?' says the Country Mouse.
'Quick! It's people! Let's run!' says the Town Mouse.

The Town Mouse and the Country Mouse run and they hide in a little hole.

The Country Mouse says, 'It's very nice food.'
But he thinks, 'It's a pity we can't eat it!'

4.2 Town Mouse and Country Mouse: introducing the story

You can use this set of activities to introduce the story if you wish. Broader topic-based work can then follow. The children act out the story and add lots of their own ideas.

LEVEL	**Elementary and pre-intermediate**
AGE	**8 to 12**
TIME	**90 minutes**
LANGUAGE	**Complimenting:** *What a nice. . . !*; **vocabulary for food; countables and uncountables**
MATERIALS	Magazine pictures of food, or real food; large paper bags and large black felt-tip pens to make the mouse masks.
PREPARATION	1 Collect magazine pictures of food and stick them on to card— the more the better.

2 Make large signs:

Loudly	Quietly	Very quietly	Stop

3 Practise drawing the pictures.

IN CLASS

1 Display the pictures of food one by one, saying the names of the types of food and alternating between countable and uncountable nouns. For example:

Here's an orange.
Here's some fruit.
Here's a banana.
Here's some milk.

2 Ask the children if they can remember the words for the pictures you have displayed. They should respond with:
That's an orange.
That's some fruit.
Do not insist on accurate use of *some/a/an* from young children.

3 Look again at the pictures and pick out a particularly nice picture. Say: *What a lovely orange!* (miming that you really do like it).

Repeat with a few other types of food. Now extend the notion of compliments to other things by complimenting the children (not just on their appearance):

What a nice jumper, Tomás!
What neat writing, Alicia!

What a lovely drawing, Miguel!

4 Invite the children to walk about complimenting each other:

What a lovely dress!
What a lovely picture!
What lovely hair!

5 Draw a mouse on the board.
Say: *What a lovely mouse!*
Draw a silhouette of a town. Point at the town and at the mouse.
Say: *He's a town mouse.*

6 Draw a line for a hill and then a mousehole.

Say: *What a nice hill! And this is a mousehole.*

Draw two mice by the hole. Tell the children that one of them is the town mouse and the other one is the country mouse. Tell the children that you are now going to tell them a story. Tell the first half of the story.

7 Now ask for volunteers to act out the story: two mice, and two children who kneel down and hold hands making a vertical circle to represent the mousehole. Then tell the first half of the story again and manipulate the two mice and get them to repeat their lines after you.

8 Divide the class into two halves. Tell them that one half of the class is the town mouse speaking and the other half is the town mouse thinking. The 'thinking' half of the class should whisper. Tell the first half of the story again. The children chorus their lines after you.

9 Draw another mouse. Draw trees and fields below him.

Say: *What a lovely mouse! He's the country mouse. He's visiting the town mouse. Here's the town mouse's house!*

Draw the house of the town mouse. Say: *What a nice house!*

10 Tell the children that the town mouse has a lot of wonderful food and drink in his house. Divide the class into groups of about five or six. Tell them to list as many types of food as they can think of. The aim is to remember more words than the other teams.

11 After four minutes, each team says how many words they have listed. They read them out and get one point for each correct kind of food.

12 Ask for volunteers to play the country mouse and the town mouse. The rest of the class play people. The 'people' should be divided into pairs and work out a two-line dialogue about food and drink and learn it so that they can mutter this in the background when you tell them to. For example:

First person: *I love fish and chips.*
Second person: *Do you? I love beefburgers and tomato ketchup.*

13 Tell the story again, and this time ask the class to call out as many of the types of food as they can when you say: *The town mouse says, 'Thank you. Now come and eat. You can have . . .'*

When they cannot think of any more kinds of food, ask all the pairs or 'people' to start speaking their dialogues at the same time. They should repeat them until you hold up the sign *quietly* and then *very quietly* and then *stop*.

You can then complete the story with the two mice saying their dialogue.

14 The children write the story in their books or folders. They can make any additions to the food list they like. They must make a lot of use of compliments:

What a nice house!
What nice food!

You might like to write key phrases or sentences on the board for the children to copy.

FOLLOW-UP 1   Choose a topic such as food, mice, homes, or town and country, and build a lesson around it using some of the ideas in the rest of this chapter.

FOLLOW-UP 2   The idea of having a voice which people hear and an inner voice which people do not hear (but is there) offers great dramatic possibilities. It is also interesting for the children to realize that we all do it all the time! Ask them to invent some dialogues based on the above story (or completely different) in which each character has an inner voice. Each character should then be played by two people: the inner voice standing just behind the outer voice.

Topic: Mice

In this sequence of activities the children explore the characteristics of fictional mice and real mice.

4.3 Mice Mastermind

LEVEL   Elementary and pre-intermediate

AGE   10 to 14

TIME   10–20 minutes

LANGUAGE   Vocabulary; spelling

IN CLASS   Introduce the topic of mice by playing a version of the game 'Mastermind' to elicit the word 'mice'. See 2.17, 'Mastermind', page 34, for how to play this game.

4.4 Do you like mice?

LEVEL   Beginners and elementary

AGE   6 to 10

TIME   20 minutes

LANGUAGE   *Do you like . . . ?*

IN CLASS   1 Ask the children *Do you like mice or do you hate mice?*
After a moment or two draw a line on the board and divide it into ten sections. Draw a smiling face with a heart at one end and an unhappy face with a crossed-out heart at the other end.

Now ask each child to draw a mouse in the section which represents how he or she feels about mice. (If this is too time-consuming, each child can write 'x' in the appropriate column.)

2 Discuss the children's reasons for liking or disliking mice. *Why do you like them or hate them? What comes into your mind when you hear the word 'mice'?*
Possible answers include:
I think they are nasty, ugly, horrible.
I am afraid of them. My mum is afraid of mice.
I think they are nice, funny.
I think they are sweet.
Use the mother tongue if necessary.

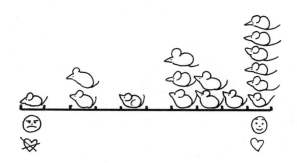

4.5 What do you know about mice?

LEVEL   Elementary and pre-intermediate

AGE   8 to 12

TIME   30 minutes

LANGUAGE   Statements in the simple present; descriptions

IN CLASS   1 Ask the children *What do you know about mice?* Brainstorm their information on the board.

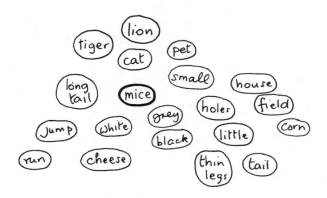

2 Play a 'true/false' game. You and/or the children make statements about mice which are either true or false based on the brainstormed information on the board. For example:

	Answers
Mice only live in the country.	False
Mice like dogs and cats.	False
Mice eat many things.	True
Mice eat everything.	True
Mice are usually afraid of people.	True
Mice are always grey.	False
Mice have short tails.	False

Photocopiable © Oxford University Press

3 Ask the class to vote for which they think are true and which they think are false. Then tell them the correct answers.

4 Write the text below on the board or photocopy it for each pair of children. Tell the children that a boy called Silly Billy has written about mice. Tell the children to give him + or − for each sentence.

	Answers
Mice only live in England.	−
Mice are usually blue and green.	−
Mice have wings.	−
Mice have long tails.	+
Mice like cheese.	+
Mice like cats and dogs.	−
Mice have got two legs.	−

Photocopiable © Oxford University Press

5 Tell the story. Pre-teach words the children don't know.

4.6 Cartoon mice

LEVEL   **Pre-intermediate**

AGE   **9 to 14**

TIME   **30 minutes**

LANGUAGE   **Questions**

IN CLASS   **1** Play 'Twenty questions' with the children. You think of Mickey Mouse, and the children can ask up to twenty questions to find out who you are thinking of. You can help the children by sketching parts of Mickey Mouse on the board.

Annotate it with *big ears, long nose, whiskers, long tail, small dark eyes, long thin legs*.

2 Show the children how to draw a cartoon mouse and let them copy it into their books.

3 Read a comic or play part of a *Tom and Jerry* video cartoon. Discuss with the children (in their mother tongue if necessary) the feelings and actions of the mouse. Eventually sketch a cartoon mouse on the board and write its characteristics around it.

4 Discuss with the children in their mother tongue if any of these characteristics are true of real mice, and the relationship between cartoon mice and humans.

5 Discuss with the children in their mother tongue whether the town mouse and the country mouse are like cartoon mice or real mice—or humans.

4.7 More mice stories

LEVEL	**All**
AGE	**7 to 10**
TIME	**20 minutes**
LANGUAGE	**Oral fluency**
IN CLASS	Ask the children if they know any other stories about mice. They could bring their books or videos to school. For example, *The Mouse and the Lion, Mighty Mouse, Speedy Gonzales, An American Tail*.

Discuss the moral of each story: 'Town mouse and country mouse': home is best. 'The mouse and the lion': even the weak can help the strong. What do the stories have in common? How are they different?

4.8 Real mice

LEVEL	**Elementary and pre-intermediate**
AGE	**8 to 13**

TIME	**60 minutes including homework**

LANGUAGE	**Descriptions of actions**

IN CLASS

1 Ask the children to find as much information as possible about mice in the school, at the public library, or at home.

2 Next lesson: Share the information gathered. Write up interesting or surprising facts on the board, for example *Mice eat candles.*

3 See the worksheet for some information which the children can study and discuss with you. What kind(s) of mouse are town mouse and country mouse? They can vote for their favourite kind of mouse.

FOLLOW-UP

If the children have mice or related animals as pets, or if the school has a mouse, gerbil, or similar animal, the children can observe its behaviour and write a 'mouse's diary'.

4.9 Mice can . . .

LEVEL	**All**

AGE	**10 to 14**

TIME	**40 minutes**

LANGUAGE	***Can* for ability**

MATERIALS	Long strips of paper about 10 cm wide

IN CLASS

1 Discuss with the children what mice and humans can do. The following language will be useful:

What can mice/humans do?
Can mice/humans . . . ?
Can mice/humans . . . very well?
Mice/humans can . . .

2 Write the children's complete sentences on the strips of paper and display them as they are completed. Write each sentence on a different strip. Possible sentences at pre-intermediate level might include: *Mice can eat holes in wood and cloth. Humans can't.*

Mice can go through small holes. Humans can't.
Mice can jump five times their body length. Humans can't.
Mice can hear very well in the night. Humans can't.
Mice can climb very well. Humans can, too.

Mice

Pygmy mouse
The pygmy mouse is the smallest mouse. It lives for one year. It lives everywhere in the world except Antarctica. It weighs six grams and is four and a half centimetres long and has a tail three centimetres long.

Jumping mouse
The jumping mouse has long back feet. The Woodland jumping mouse can jump three metres. Jumping mice sleep for six to nine months in the year. They eat seeds, worms, and beetles.

House mouse
The house mouse lives with people. It eats anything it can find. It can eat soap and glue and electricity cables. They are popular pets.

Harvest mouse
The harvest mouse can climb very well. It climbs grass and corn and holds on with its tail. It makes its nest at the top of stalks of grass and corn.

Dormouse
Small dormice are six centimetres long and weigh fifteen grams, and big ones are nineteen centimetres long and weigh two hundred grams. They sleep for seven months every year. They live for about three years. Dormice can hear very well and can make a lot of noises. They eat fruit, nuts, seeds, insects, spiders, worms, and eggs. The Romans liked to eat dormice.

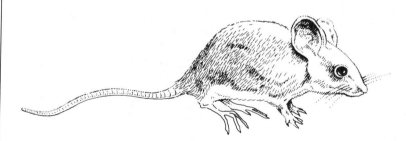

The oldest mouse was a house mouse who lived for five years and eleven months. He was called Hercules.

The largest number of baby mice born at one time from one mother was thirty-two.

The greatest enemy of mice was a cat called Mickey who killed more than twenty-two thousand in his twenty-three years of life.

Humans can speak languages. Mice can't.
Humans can write. Mice can't.
Humans can make music. Mice can't.
Humans can laugh. Mice can't.
Humans can invent things. Mice can't.
Humans can destroy the planet. Mice can't.

3 Ask the children to list all the sentences in their books and to add any others they wish. The page should have a title, for example *Of Mice and Men* (the title of John Steinbeck's story!) and should have an illustration of mice at the top.

4 Ask the children to choose three sentences and illustrate them decoratively on the page, but not next to the sentences. They should a give number or a letter to each illustration.

5 The children should then go to other children, asking them to look at the illustrations and to guess which sentence they are supposed to illustrate. See which children get the most people guessing correctly. Here is a possible survey form completed by one child:

Name	Picture	Sentences
Timea	A	Humans can make music.
Susan	B	Mice can get through small holes.
Julia	C	Mice can jump five times their body length.

6 Ask the children again what they think of mice. Has their opinion about mice changed?

Topic: Home

4.10 Find your way home

LEVEL	Elementary
AGE	8 to 12
TIME	20 minutes
LANGUAGE	Directions
PREPARATION	Photocopy the map: one for each child. Photocopy the instructions below, one for each pair of children.
IN CLASS	**1** Tell the children that they must help the Town Mouse and the Country Mouse to find their way home!

2 Divide the children into pairs.

3 Give all the children a map, and give one child in each pair the instructions for the Country Mouse and the other child the instructions for the Town Mouse.

4 The children take it in turns to give instructions to the other mouse on how to get home. The mice can draw in the route that they take.

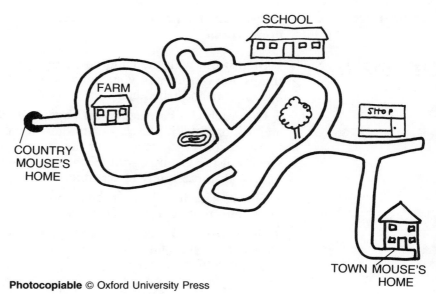

This way for the Town Mouse

Go to the farm and turn right. Go to the pond and continue straight on. Go to the school and turn right. Go to the big tree and turn left. Go to the shop and turn right. Go straight on and there is your home!

This way for the Country Mouse

Go to the shop and turn left. Go to the big tree and turn right. Go to the school and turn left. Go to the pond and continue straight on. Go to the farm and turn left. Go straight on and there is your home.

Photocopiable © Oxford University Press

FOLLOW-UP

The children can design their own maps and instructions based on the ones given here.

4.11 Furnishing a home

LEVEL

Elementary

AGE

7 to 12

TIME

30 minutes

LANGUAGE

Vocabulary for furniture etc.; descriptions; *There is*; prepositions

IN CLASS

1 Brainstorm with the children all the words they know for things you can have in your home: bed, table, clock, toys, books, pots and pans, etc.

2 Give each child a piece of A4 paper. Divide the class into pairs and ask one child in each pair to draw a cross-section of the house of the Town Mouse and the other child to make a cross section of the Country Mouse's house. Ask them to furnish their houses as interestingly as possible.

3 Now ask each child to make a copy of the outline of their house and to give it to their partner.

4 Each partner then describes his or her house and its contents so that the other child can draw the contents into the same places as in the first child's drawing.

There is a table in the middle of the room.

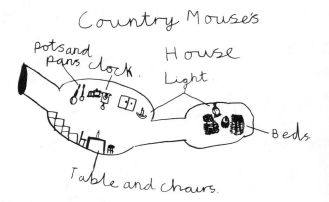

There is a clock on the wall above the table.
There is a light next to the beds.

5 When the 'picture dictation' is done, the children can compare drawings to see how accurate they were.

4.12 Types of home

LEVEL	**Elementary and pre-intermediate**
AGE	**8 to 14**
TIME	**20 minutes**
LANGUAGE	**'Home' vocabulary; cultural awareness**
PREPARATION	Collect as many pictures of homes as you can, for example: detached house, block of flats, terrace house, bungalow, cottage, farmhouse, hotel, tent, caravan, castle, houseboat, motel, camper van, palace, teepee.
	Include homes from other countries.
IN CLASS	1 Identify each one with the children and make a display. The children can write their name under the sort of home they live in.
	2 Discuss with the children, in their mother tongue if necessary, what we need from a home (shelter from the weather, privacy, a place to put things, a place we feel is ours). Discuss the advantages and disadvantages of each type of home.
	3 Talk about the sort of homes people used to live in and how technology has changed homes (electricity, gas, sewers).

4.13 Dream home

LEVEL	**All**
AGE	**6 to 14**
TIME	**30 minutes**
LANGUAGE	**'Home' vocabulary**

IN CLASS

1 Ask the children to draw and annotate their 'dream home'. They must take into account all their needs and write next to their picture how each part of their design fulfils their need. They should draw a cross section and a plan.

2 Continue by asking them to be architects for other people: very rich people without children; very poor people with a lot of children; people in cold countries; people in hot countries; or people in wet countries. In each case they should describe what the people need and then show how their design answers their needs.

FOLLOW-UP

The children design imaginary homes for animals.

4.14 Animals' homes

LEVEL	**Elementary and pre-intermediate**
AGE	**5 to 14 (depending on the amount of detail)**
TIME	**40 minutes**
LANGUAGE	**Vocabulary of animals and their habitats**

PREPARATION

Collect pictures of real animals' homes.

IN CLASS

1 Encourage the children to bring pictures of animals' homes. They draw more examples and make a display.

2 Ask the children if animals have homes in the same way as humans. For example, do birds feel that their nest is their home, or is it just a place where the eggs are laid and the chicks grow until they fly? Some birds return to the same nest year after year (for example, swallows). Some birds sleep in the same trees all their lives. Many animals sleep and bring up their families in the same holes or caves.
Useful words in English include: nest, eggs (bird), cave (bear or bat), hole (mouse or rabbit), earth (fox), sett (badger).

In your discussion with the children, distinguish between
'homes' made by the animals and 'homes' made by people, for
example, stable (horse), cowshed (cow), pigsty (pig), kennel
(dog), tank (fish), hutch (rabbit or guinea-pig), cage (mouse or
bird).

3 The discussion might also include the importance of habitat.
For example, pandas are dying out because people cut down
bamboo forests. If the coral reefs in warm seas disappear,
millions of fish and other creatures will die. Many of the fish live
in one very small area and sleep in one particular hole in the
coral.

4.15 True/false

LEVEL   Elementary and pre-intermediate

AGE   9 to 12

TIME   15 minutes

LANGUAGE   Animal vocabulary; statements in the present simple

IN CLASS   **1** Make a series of statements which are true or false. The
children repeat the sentences which are true and remain silent
when they hear a false one.

Examples

Birds live in nests.
People live in tanks.
Cows live in stables.
Fish live in tanks.

2 Instead of remaining silent when they hear a false sentence,
ask the children to correct you.

People don't live in tanks; they live in houses.

4.16 Rhymes

LEVEL   Elementary and pre-intermediate

AGE   10 to 14

TIME   30 minutes

LANGUAGE   **Extending vocabulary and written fluency; pronunciation**

IN CLASS   1 Brainstorm on to the board words which rhyme with the words for animals.

Examples

fish–dish, mice–ice, mouse–house, cat–flat–hat, frog–dog, cock–sock, hare–air–hair, shark–dark.

2 Ask the children to make rhymes with these rhyming words.

Example

The big, fat mice
Live in the cold, blue ice.

Topic: Town and country

In this sequence of activities the children explore the differences between life in the town and the country from the point of view of the Town Mouse and the Country Mouse, and also from their own point of view.

4.17 Town Mastermind

IN CLASS   Introduce the topic of town and country by playing a version of the game 'Mastermind' to elicit the word 'town'. (See 2.17 and 4.3 for how to play this game.)

4.18 Town and country poems

LEVEL   All

AGE   8 to 12

TIME   45 minutes

LANGUAGE   Vocabulary: town, country, and associations

MATERIALS   A large number of magazine pictures which illustrate aspects of town and country.

IN CLASS

1 Put the pictures on your table. Ask children to come and select a picture, hold it up for the class to see, and to say whether it illustrates the town or the country. Display the pictures in three groups: town, country, town and country.

2 Select a picture from the town group and one from the country group. Display them on the board. Ask the children to call out what they associate with each picture. Write summary words or phrases of what they say in bubbles on the board (see 4.5, 'What do you know about mice?' page 156).

3 Now ask the children to call out a single word that they associate with any of the words in the bubbles. For example, *policeman–criminal, road–noise, flats–house*. Ask the children who are volunteering the associations to add their idea in a bubble and to join it to the idea they associate it with.

4 Erase the words from inside the bubbles. Now ask the children to try to remember the words or phrases you have erased and to write them back again.

5 Ask the children to make up 'town' and 'country' poems from the words they have put in bubbles on the board. For the town the poem might be:

> People everywhere
> People in the houses
> People in the streets
> People in the shops
> People walking and running
> Talking and laughing
> Crying and thinking
> People everywhere.

For the country the poem might be:

> Trees and flowers
> Leaves and grass

Cows and goats
Geese and hens
Sun, wind, and rain.

4.19 Town or country?

LEVEL	**Elementary**
AGE	**8 to 12**
TIME	**20 minutes**
LANGUAGE	**Likes and dislikes; descriptions**
IN CLASS	**1** Ask children whether they prefer the country or the town.

1 Ask children whether they prefer the country or the town.

2 Ask them to get into groups and become country mice or town mice, according to their preference.

3 They should make a list of all the good things about the place they like and all the bad things about the place they don't like.

4 The children should then compare their lists with the other groups' lists.

Examples

Here is a list made by a country mouse contrasted with that of a town mouse.

Country mouse   Town mouse
I like the country because: I don't like the country because:

It is very quiet.   It is very quiet.
It is not very dangerous.   It is boring.
It is beautiful.   There are no people.
It is interesting   There is nothing to do.
It is very clean.   It is very dirty.
                                       It is dangerous. There are no
                                       hospitals there.

5 Discuss the lists of points with the class and point out that for many people and mice the same thing can be either good or bad!

4.20 Letters

LEVEL — **Pre-intermediate**

AGE — **10 to 14**

TIME — **30–40 minutes**

LANGUAGE — **Writing letters; descriptions; *can***

IN CLASS — **1** Divide the class into town mice and country mice.

2 Ask them to write a letter to their friend in the country or the town and to say why they like where they live. List useful phrases and words on the board.

I live in a hole/house/hotel/school.
It is very small/comfortable/safe/warm/clean.
I can hear/see/smell . . .
I feel happy/sad/good/bad/excited/frightened/bored.
I can walk/run/swim/go to the shops/go to the cinema/go to the disco.
I can eat nuts/fruit/vegetables/cheese/meat.
I can have lots of friends.

3 Every mouse receives a letter and replies to it, saying why he or she doesn't like the home of the other mouse.

4.21 Town and country descriptions

LEVEL — **Pre-intermediate, perhaps elementary**

AGE — **10 to 14**

TIME — **20 minutes**

LANGUAGE — **Descriptions**

IN CLASS — **1** Display one picture representing the country and one representing the town. Fix an envelope next to each picture.

2 Read out sentences which describe the country or the town (they could be extracts from letters). Ask the children to decide which is which and ask them to put them into the appropriate envelope. Here are some examples of sentences you might use:

In the mornings I can hear the birds singing in the woods.
I like walking in the park and looking at the flowers.
From my window I can see lots of cars, buses, and lorries in the streets.
It is very quiet.
There are lots of discos, cinemas, and cafés.

VARIATION Instead of you producing the sentences, you can ask children at pre-intermediate level to write sentences which they then read out. The class decide which envelope the sentence should go in. After everybody has read out one sentence, count them up and find how many sentences there are in the country envelope and how many in the town envelope.

4.22 Town and country display

LEVEL All

TIME 45 minutes +

AGE Any

LANGUAGE Revision of town and country language

IN CLASS The children collect pictures and objects to make a display contrasting life in the town and in the country.

This could include:

- walks in the town and country to collect materials and take photos
- pictures from magazines, calendars, or holiday brochures
- children's drawings and collages
- written work including that done in 4.18, 'Town and country poems', 4.19 'Town or country?', and 4.20 'Letters'.

5 Grammar and stories

Stories are an excellent way to introduce language that learners are not yet familiar with, be it a point of grammar, a function, an area of vocabulary, or pronunciation. Stories present language in a context that is easy to understand. They can be told again and again, and thus the language point can be repeated again and again, each time in a meaningful context. The language items new to the child are experienced as part of the fabric of meaning, and this invites the child to hypothesize on the meaning offered by the new item within that fabric.

The teaching of grammar to young learners is contentious. Even if explicit grammatical references are made, it is generally agreed that the children must first of all have a rich experience of the grammatical items used in a meaningful way. Young children do not analyse language, and new grammatical items are first learnt as 'lexical chunks'. This is the best way to introduce the simple past tense, for example: the story is a natural vehicle for exposure to past tenses, which can later be turned into active use. It is best to use a topic- or activity-centred approach to language learning in the primary years, introducing new language elements in a meaningful context when the children are ready for them. Stories are ideal for this.

The current consensus of opinion is that the explicit teaching of grammar should only take place with older children at the pre-intermediate level. From the age of 10 or 11, you can actively encourage learners to start hypothesizing about why we say things the way we do. For example, from 'The little white cat' (3.6), learners could draw conclusions about English word order:

> She jumps into the bag and then she jumps out of the bag.
> 'You are so black! Now you are a little black cat!'

(Which comes first in English: the adjective or the noun? The preposition or the noun?)

or about singular and plural forms:

> 'Hello, witch. Have you got a cat?'
> 'No, I haven't got a cat.'
> 'Well, I'm your cat!' says the little white cat.
> 'No, you're not! You're white. Witches have black cats.'

(Ask the children to notice the singular and plural forms of the nouns and then to hypothesize about how the plural is formed in English.)

A word of warning: children must not feel that they are being given stories to sugar the pill of unpleasant grammar! Don't spoil the quality of the story, and don't lose the children's trust and goodwill towards the use of stories in your lessons!

5.1 Making a pattern book

LEVEL   **Elementary**

AGE   **9 to 13**

TIME   **60 minutes**

LANGUAGE   **Sentence patterns you want the children to practise**

MATERIALS   A piece of paper for each child

PREPARATION   1 Choose a story which is based on a sentence pattern which you would like the children to practise. The children should have heard and worked on the story before (see the activities given with the stories and in Chapter 2, 'A store of 94 activities'). Here I use 3.3, 'The little duckling', as an example.

2 Fold the pieces of paper as shown to make a concertina book for each child. If you prefer the children can do this themselves in class at Step 3. Make one for yourself to show them.

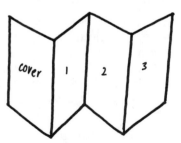

IN CLASS   1 Ask the children to try to remember the story you have chosen and to retell it to you. As they do so try to steer them to remembering the pattern which is repeated in the story. Write this on the board:

The little duckling sees a peacock.
'What a beautiful tail! I want a tail like that!'
Suddenly, the little duckling has a big beautiful peacock's tail!
The little duckling is very pleased.

2 Show the children how to invent a new character in place of the little duckling, and new wishes that it might have, for example:

The big tiger sees an elephant.
'What a beautiful trunk! I want a trunk like that!'

Suddenly, the big tiger has a beautiful trunk.
The big tiger is very pleased.

Here is another, rather more eccentric variation:

The big bus sees a chocolate birthday cake.
'What beautiful chocolate! I want chocolate like that!'
Suddenly, the big bus has a beautiful chocolate top.
The big bus is very pleased.

3 When you are sure that the children can invent characters of their own and wishes for them, show them the concertina book and explain that:

- the first page will be the cover of their book
- the next two pages will be the different wishes of their animal/object
- the last page will be the end of their story.

The children might like to cut the tops of their pages to make the shape of their picture (see page 197).

Other patterns which the children can use to create more pattern stories include:

- Going from big to small locations (see 3.2, 'In a dark, dark town', page 78):
  In a dark, dark town
  There is a dark, dark road.

- A person or animal going for a walk (see 3.4, 'The little Indian boy', page 84):
  He walks along the road.
  He runs down the hill.

- An animal looking for its mother/friend:
  'Where's my mummy/friend?'
  'I don't know. Go to the station!'

VARIATION

A longer concertina book can be used to make the story longer. The children might work together in pairs or groups.

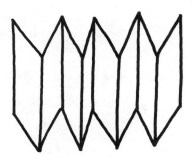

COMMENTS

Almost any sentence pattern can provide the basis for a story, but remember that for a true story you will need some kind of 'problem' and some kind of resolution at the end, or it will just remain a description!

5.2 Half sentences

LEVEL	**Elementary and pre-intermediate**
AGE	**10 to 14**
TIME	**The whole suggested sequence of steps takes 40 minutes**
LANGUAGE	**Syntax and putting sentences in order; listening comprehension and reading aloud**
PREPARATION	**1** Choose any story which can be reasonably summarized by half the number of sentences as there are children in the class. For example, if there are 30 children in the class, you will take 15 key sentences of the story. The story may be new or known to the children.

2 Write the key sentences on slips of paper. Cut the sentences into two pieces, taking into account that the children must try to find the other part of the sentence and match it up.
Examples of sentences taken from 3.6, 'The little white cat' (page 92):

The little white cat has	six black brothers and sisters.
The little white cat doesn't know	that she is white.
I'm going to be	a witch's cat!
The little white cat looks for a	witch.
Witches have	black cats.
Go	away!
She is so sad	and so hungry.
At last she comes to	a cottage.
I'm so weak and	I'm so hungry.
She jumps into the bag	and then she jumps out of the bag.
Now you are	a little black cat!
That's good because	I am going to be a witch's cat!
She is sitting	in the rocking chair in the front door.
Oh, you are	a nice little cat!
What a pity, I can't see you	because I'm blind.

Photocopiable © Oxford University Press

The sentences 'Witches have black cats.' and 'Go away!' occur twice in the story. Either ask children with these sentences to read them twice, or make two copies of them.

IN CLASS

1 Read or tell the story you have chosen. If the children have not heard the story before, prepare them for it in the usual way (see Chapter 2). The full story of 'The little white cat' is on page 92.

2 Give each child a slip of paper with a half sentence on it. Explain that each child has got half a sentence from the story. The children should look at their half sentences carefully and try to imagine (and maybe write down) what the other half of their sentence might be.

3 Tell the children that you are going to read the story again (i.e. the summary of the story made by the selected sentences in this activity) and they should raise their hand or stand up when they hear their half sentence. Tell them to watch carefully to see who has the half sentence which belongs to theirs.

4 Tell them to join the child with the half sentence which belongs to theirs. Ask which children were able to predict the other half of their sentence. The children may not have noticed which child has the other part of their sentence. In this case they should walk around, reading out their half sentence until they find their partner.

5 Tell them that you will read the story again and that each pair should listen out for their sentence and put up their hands when they hear it. They should then listen out for the sentences which come immediately before and after theirs and note which children have them.

6 Tell the children that they will stand in a big circle in order to tell the story. Begin to tell the story. As soon as the children hear their sentences they should come to stand in the circle in the correct sequence.

7 Make sure that all the children are standing in the correct sequence. Then ask them to read their half sentences in order, clearly and slowly so that the whole story can be told.

8 Do this two or three times until the children can read the sentences efficiently, and then tape-record it and play it back to them.

COMMENTS

This activity can be applied to most stories which can be summarized in ten to fifteen sentences. It engages the children in the demanding task of trying to sort out the sequence of the sentences to make the story.

5.3 Sticky story

LEVEL	**Pre-intermediate**
AGE	**10 to 14**
TIME	**45 minutes if all the steps in the sequence are followed**
LANGUAGE	**Punctuation, spelling, reading, and writing for meaning**
MATERIALS	If you want to do all the suggested steps, get a long strip of paper and a broad-tipped pen for each sentence selected from the story.
PREPARATION	**1** Copy a story without punctuation or gaps between words. Write each sentence on a separate piece of paper or card. The example below is from 3.11, 'The bottom of the sea' (page 120).
	2 Photocopy the illustration on page 122 for each pair of children, or copy it on to a large piece of paper.

The key words illustrated are:

> king   sea   tower   weeds   stones
> dirty   fish   sick   sad
> clean   fins   trash   cans
> sea-horse   eels   dolphins   starfish   crabs
> paper   plastic bottles   old tins   shoes
> coral reefs
> party   whale
> keyboard   violin   trumpet

IN CLASS	**1** Pre-teach the key words which you can illustrate and then read the story twice.

2 Divide up the class into pairs or groups. Give each group the same number of sentences (or about the same amount of text) to work on. The sentences should be in random order.

3 Decipher a sample sentence with the whole class. Then tell the children to decipher their sentences and rewrite them with the appropriate punctuation in their exercise books, or on to long strips of paper with the broad felt-tip pens. Some children may need a lot of help with this. They can do it in pairs or small groups.

4 When all the pairs are ready, ask them to think at which point their sentence(s) might be in the story: towards the beginning, middle, or end.

5 If the children have written their sentences on long strips of paper they should now try to arrange themselves and their sentences in order around the class in a big circle.

itistheyear2010

kingtritonlivesatthebottomoftheseainanivorytoweramongweed
sandlittlestones

theseaisverydirtyandkingtritonandallthefishareverysickandsad

ohdearohdearwhatcanwedosaysonelittlefish

dontworrythekingsaysthefishcanclearthewaterwiththeirfins
andthetrashcanscaneatallthetrash

sothemulticolouredfishtheseahorsestheeelsthesharksthe
dolphinsthestarfishandthecrabscleanandcleanandcleanthesea

thetrashcanseatallthetrashallthepaperplasticbagsandplastic
bottlestheoldtinsandshoes

finallyaftertwentyfivedaystheyfinishthework

thewateriscleanandtransparenttheseaweedisgreenandthe
coralreefsarepink

kingtritonandthefisharenotsicknow

kingtritoninvitesallthefishtoapartyat630pminthewhalesmouth

aneelplaysthekeyboardtheseahorsesplaytheviolinsthe
dolphinsplaythetrumpets

sebastianthelittlecrabconductstheorchestratheyalllivehappily
everafter

Photocopiable © Oxford University Press

6 Now read out the story again. If the children have written
their sentences in their exercise books, they can hold up their
hands when they hear their sentences. If the children are
standing in a circle with their sentence strips, all the class can
check the accuracy of the sequencing and ask children who are in
the wrong order to get into the proper place!

7 Finally, ask some of the children to read out the story again,
or each pair to read their sentence in sequence.

5.4 Who am I?

LEVEL	**Pre-intermediate**
AGE	**10–14**
TIME	**30 minutes**
LANGUAGE	**Question forms such as** *did you . . . ?*, *have you got . . . ?*

MATERIALS   Two small pieces of card (A6) for each child.

IN CLASS   **1** Brainstorm with the children on to the board all the names of characters from stories they can think of. They can suggest characters from modern films or television series as well as from traditional stories: James Bond, Little Red Riding Hood, etc.

2 They should then brainstorm with you what completed action in the past (simple past tense form) each character in their story might be associated with, what they wear, etc.

3 Play a guessing game. One child thinks of one of the characters. The other children call out questions, for example, *Did you kill a giant?*

If the children prepare as much information about the character as they can think of, then a much wider range of questions can be asked, for example, *Have you got a hen?*

5.5 Story dominoes

LEVEL   **Pre-intermediate and above**

AGE   **11 +**

TIME   **40 minutes**

LANGUAGE   **Simple past tense**

PREPARATION   **1** This activity depends on the children being familiar with at least two stories or fairy tales in English or in their mother tongue.

2 Divide two A4 sheets into eight pieces each. These will be the dominoes. Select nouns from stories the children are familiar with. Write one noun on the right of each domino and one noun on the left side. On each domino the nouns at each end must be from different stories. It's a good idea to make some quick drafts of the dominoes and to try them out yourself to make sure that they will match when the game is played.

The sample nouns below are selected from stories in this book: 'Little Red Riding Hood' (3.7), 'The little white cat' (3.6), 'Elidor' (3.13), and 'Ma Liang' (3.8). Of course, your children must be familiar with these four stories if you want to use this particular selection. (If they don't know these stories you must make up your own pairs of nouns from stories they do know.)

3 Photocopy the A4 sheets, making one copy of each sheet for each group of four children, i.e. one set for each group.

4 Now cut up the A4 sheets into 16 dominoes.

soot	Ma Liang	Ma Liang	wolf
Little Red Riding Hood	China	cottage	Elidor
witch	hen	Elidor	king
prison	grandmother's cottage	golden ball	Chinese girl
Chinese girl	sandwiches	girl	hole
prince	rocking chair	wolf	knee
basket	school	brush	witch
horse	little white cat	river	chimney sweep

Photocopiable © Oxford University Press

IN CLASS

1 Write two of the nouns from the same story on the board. Ask the class to suggest what the connection might be. (Note: the children might need a list of verbs which can be used with the nouns on the board. You might provide this list or you might compile it with the children.)

Tell them to use the past tense when making the connection between the nouns if they are familiar with it—otherwise use the present.

Example

basket/cottage
The children might say: *Little Red Riding Hood took the basket to grandmother's cottage.*

Continue to give some more examples until you and the children are confident that they know what to do.

2 Now write a number of nouns in muddled order on the board from different stories, but make sure some of them are from the same story.

Example

Elidor soot wolf hole chimney sweep forest

The children think of connections between the words, for example:

Elidor climbed through the hole.
The chimney sweep had some soot.
The wolf was in the forest.

Write some examples on the board for the children to refer to during the game.

3 If you are confident that all the children in the class will be able to cope, tell the class they are going to play a game of story dominoes. Put the children in groups of four. Give each child four domino cards. On each domino there are two words from stories the children know. Tell the children what the stories are. If you think some of them might not remember the stories very clearly then elicit the gist, in their mother tongue if necessary. Explain the basic rules of dominoes, i.e. the children take it in turns to lay down a domino, connecting two words from the same story. The children must say a sentence combining the two words, as in the examples on the board. If the group think the sentence is correct and relevant to the story then the child can leave the domino on the table. If it is not correct or relevant, or the child cannot make a connection, then he or she must pick it up again and wait for another turn.

The winner is the child who puts down all his or her domino cards first.

COMMENTS

This is a difficult activity involving the children in trying to find connections between two words and explaining that connection in a coherent sentence, but I have kept it in the book for those teachers and children who can cope with it!

5.6 Houses into bricks; bricks into houses

LEVEL

Pre-intermediate

AGE

12 +

TIME

40 minutes + homework

LANGUAGE

Developing the children's appreciation of grammatical groupings of words and their relationships within sentences

PREPARATION

1 Decide which grammatical groupings you would like the children to become aware of.

2 Select a story and pick out five to ten sentences from it which exemplify the main grammatical groupings you have chosen. Alternatively, make use of the sentences below taken from 'Little Red Riding Hood' (3.7, page 96).

There are sandwiches and there is cake in the basket.
There is a wolf in the forest and it is very dangerous.
She likes flowers and she picks them.
She lives in a cottage in the wood.
The wolf goes into the cottage and eats the grandmother.

Little Red Riding Hood dances and sings in the forest.
She looks at the wolf in bed.

IN CLASS

1 Write a sentence, for example, *Little Red Riding Hood dances and sings in the forest*, on the board.
Draw four big, empty bags on the board and label them with the grammatical groupings you want to practise.

2 Ask *Who dances and sings?* Write *Little Red Riding Hood* in the first bag.

Ask *Where does she dance?* Write the noun *forest* in the second bag.

Ask *What does she do?* Write the verbs *dances, sings* in the third bag.

Write the other words in the remaining bag: *and, in, the*

3 Write another sentence on the board, for example, *She lives in a cottage in the wood*. Ask the children to help you put the words in the right bags on the board. Do this with several more sentences.

4 Write some more sentences on the board. Ask the children to work in pairs and to discuss which bag they should put each word in.

5 As a class, discuss which words in the remaining sentences go into which bags, and write them in.

6 Explain to the children that they have taken the sentences to pieces and now they can use the same pieces to make a new story. It is a little bit like taking a Lego house to pieces and putting each type of Lego brick together so that it is easy to find what you want if you make something else.

7 The children should now make a copy of the four bags and their contents. They should write a new story about Little Red Riding Hood using some of the words in the bags and any others they wish.

8 When they have written their story they should list all the proper nouns, common nouns, and verbs they have used.

9 When the stories have been written, pairs can exchange stories, analyse them into the bags of words, and then see how these groupings compare with the groupings of the children who wrote the story.

COMMENTS

1 Many children are not helped by an explicit teaching of grammar. This activity is not teaching, in the sense of telling, but teaching in the sense of helping children to use their natural abilities to look for meaningful relationships and to hypothesize about them. This kind of activity helps to make children active and responsible in their acquisition of grammatical generalizations.

2 It is not necessary to give grammatical names to the categories. You may judge that this is inappropriate for children. You can also use colours to distinguish the different types of word—see *Young Learners* in this series, page 83.

5.7 Gapped texts

LEVEL

Pre-intermediate

AGE

12 +

TIME

40 minutes

LANGUAGE

Vocabulary reinforcement; syntax

PREPARATION

Take a text, remove some of the words, and make enough copies for all the students. You might like to use the example on the next page by photocopying it.

IN CLASS

1 Tell the story.
2 The children write the correct words in the gaps.

VARIATION 1

Depending on the proficiency and competence of your children you may like to do this activity as a whole-class activity in which all the children have a copy of the gapped text and you sort out with the children what should be written into the gaps. All the children should complete their own copy.

VARIATION 2

A harder version of this activity is to keep all the missing words in the correct order, but run them together as in 5.3, 'Sticky story'.

FOLLOW-UP

The children can now prepare their own gapped text and give it to another group or class. In the act of preparing the text the children will learn something about the language feature they are focusing on.

The little duckling

The little _____ sees a _____.

'What a beautiful _____! I want a beautiful _____ too!'

Suddenly the little _____ has a big, beautiful _____'s _____!

The little _____ is very pleased.

The little _____ sees a _____.

'What beautiful _____! I want beautiful _____, too!'

Suddenly the little _____ has long, thin, pink _____!'

The little _____ is very pleased.

The little _____ sees an _____.

'What beautiful _____ I want beautiful _____, too!'

Suddenly, the little _____ has big, brown _____!

The little _____ is very pleased.

The little _____ sees a _____.

'What a beautiful _____! I want a beautiful _____, too!'

Suddenly, the little _____ has a big, red, handsome _____!

The little _____ is very pleased.

All the little _____'s _____ swim in the _____.

The little _____ says, 'Stop! Wait for me!'

And he jumps into the _____.

But his _____'s _____ is very heavy.

His big, brown _____ are very heavy.

His long, thin, pink _____ cannot swim.

His handsome red _____ is very heavy and he can't breathe.

'Glug! Glug! Glug!

I want a little duckling's _____, and a little _____'s _____

and _____, and I don't want a _____!'

Suddenly the little _____ can swim. And he can swim very well. Soon he is with

his _____.

tail duckling duckling tail wings duckling legs legs river duckling peacock duckling
friends duckling eagle flamingo peacock wings wings wings duckling legs friends hat hat
duckling hat cock duckling duckling peacock tail duckling hat duckling tail wings
duckling legs water hat duckling tail legs duckling duckling

COMMENTS

1 As the activity is quite demanding I have taken a story previously included as suitable for beginners to make it as easy as possible. The choice and number of words you omit determine which proficiency level the activity is suitable for.

2 The gaps you leave in the text can either be random or focused on a feature of the language. In the example given here the focus is on the vocabulary of animals and their body parts. Language features which you might practise with the children at the lower levels of proficiency include nouns, adverbs, adjectives, and connectors. The broad family of 'gapped text' activities normally means exactly that: a text with gaps in it, perhaps with all the missing words listed at the bottom of the text. You can join the missing words together to add a further challenge, but this is not essential. For other examples see 2.27, 'Gapped story', 2.49 'Gap filling', and 2.50 'Information gap filling'.

5.8 Forest news

LEVEL   Elementary and pre-intermediate

AGE   10 to 14

TIME   60 minutes

LANGUAGE   Questions and answers

MATERIALS   A piece of A4 paper for each child

PREPARATION

1 The children must be familiar with at least one story and know the characters in the story.

2 Make up a copy of *Forest News* based on the example on the next page. It should be on a piece of A4 paper folded to A5.

3 If possible make a mask to show who the child in Step 3 of 'In class' is representing. For example, draw a face on a large paper bag and cut out eye holes and a mouth hole.

Forest News

WOLF EATS GIRLS!

At 10 a.m. on Saturday morning Little Red Riding Hood met a wolf in the forest. The wolf ate her. The wolf said, 'My favourite food is girls! Most girls are nice. They wash!' Wolf is thirty eight years old. He has twenty brothers and sisters and they all like girls. They live in the forest and wait for their favourite food – girls!

Strange Animal likes Dancing!

Sipo, aged fourteen, went to the cliffs and saw a strange animal. This is his picture of it.

Sipo says, 'Don't be frightened! Take a drum! It likes dancing!

ADVERTISEMENT!
Do you want good teeth? My shop is open every day. New teeth! Old teeth. Rabbit Shop. Little Hill.

IN CLASS

1 Ask the children to call out the titles of stories they know. Write them on the board.

2 Ask the children to call out the names of characters in the stories. Write them on the board.

3 Ask for a volunteer to pretend to be one of the characters and to sit at the front of the class (or wherever all the children can see her or him) and answer questions as if they were that character. The child puts on the mask (see Preparation).

4 Help the class to ask the story character as many questions as possible. (The questions should not relate directly to the story itself.) The child pretending to be the story character must invent and give her or his answers. Write each of the questions on the board. Here are the sort of questions the class might ask:

What's your name?
How old are you?
Have you got any brothers or sisters?
Where do you live?
Who are your friends?
What do you do with your friends?
What is your favourite food?
What are your favourite television programmes?
What is your favourite music?
What are your hobbies?

5 Ask the children to choose a character from any of the stories for themselves, draw their character in their exercise books, write down the questions you have written on the board, and to write their character's answers.

6 Divide the class into pairs of different characters. Each child takes it in turns to be a reporter for the local newspaper, the *Forest News*, and the character being interviewed. The interviewer can be guided by the questions on the board.

The interviewer must note down the answers to her or his questions.

7 Now show the children the copy of *Forest News* you have made. Point out how big the letters for the title must be. Also point out how it is arranged in columns: the pictures they draw and the lines they write must be the same width. (You might like to make this work part of a more general study of graphic design in newspapers and books.)

8 The children should now make their own copy of *Forest News* and write up their interview without referring to the questions. They should give a title to their article. The children should also do a drawing of the most important piece of information. For example:

```
Wolf Eats Girls

'My favourite food is girls!' says Wolf.
'Most girls are nice. They wash. Boys are
not very nice. They don't wash.'

Wolf is thirty-eight years old. He has
twenty brothers and sisters and they all
like girls. They live in the forest ...
```

If this is too difficult, the children can just concentrate on copying out the basic answers they received to their questions. You might even give them a model text on the board so they only have to substitute the special information which they have. The children can write the text in pencil first then show it to you and correct it if necessary, before writing it up neatly in pen or typing it out. If your school has a computer, they can write and edit their text on this.

9 Let the children walk about trying to find someone else who has written about the same character. They should then compare the information.

10 With the whole class, compare information on the same character, so that the other children can hear what the differences are. If there are differences, ask the class, for example, *Do you think Wolf is thirty-eight or sixty-four?*

5.9 Asking questions

LEVEL	Elementary and pre-intermediate
AGE	10 to 14
TIME	20 minutes
LANGUAGE	Questions; oral fluency

PREPARATION

1 You need to choose a story which you don't mind being interrupted! It should be a short story. Here are some stories which I have used: 'In a dark, dark town' (3.2, page 77); 'Father, son, and donkey' (3.5, page 88); 'Ghosts' (6.8, page 196); 'The donkey and the little dog' (6.4, page 193); 'The fox and the crow' (6.7, page 195); 'The boy who cried wolf' (6.6, page 194); 'The travellers and the bear' (6.16, page 204).

IN CLASS

1 Tell the children the story. Then comment that it is a very short story and invite the children to ask you questions about it.

2 Tell them that you are going to play a game with them. Say you are going to tell the story again in less than five minutes, and they must try to stop you from finishing the story by asking questions.

3 Help the class to think of all the different kinds of questions they can ask in order to find out more information. Write some examples on the board. Here are some questions which could be asked about 'In a dark, dark town' (3.2):

Is it very dark?
Can you see the houses?
What time is it?
Is it raining?
What day is it?
Where is this town?
What is the name of the town?
Is it a big town?
Are there trees in the road?
Are there any cars?

Is it a big road?
Who lives in the house?
How old is he or she?
What are his or her hobbies?
What colour is the front door?

4 Tell the story, pausing at the end of each line to give the children a chance to call out a question. Encourage shy and less fluent children to ask questions. Give the impression that you are desperate to tell the story so try to give short answers.

The class win if they can prevent you from completing the story in five minutes.

FOLLOW-UP

With higher-level classes try this game on another occasion, without helping the children to prepare questions beforehand.

COMMENTS

This activity requires the children to think quickly and be willing to call out their questions. It is not easy but nevertheless gives an opportunity for the children to develop their willingness to 'have a go'.

6 More stories and ideas

In this section I have included extra stories and brief suggestions for activities in class. You can also choose suitable activities from Chapter 2, 'A store of 94 activities'.

Beginners

6.1 The monkeys

There are two young monkeys in a tree. Crunchy has a banana.
Munchy is angry.
Munchy: 'That's my banana!'
Crunchy: 'No, it isn't.'
Munchy: 'That's my banana! Give it to me!'
Crunchy: 'No, it isn't and I won't.'
Munchy: 'Give it to me!'
Crunchy: 'No, I won't!'
Elephant: 'Give it to me! . . . Thank you!'

The elephant takes the banana.

Munchy: 'OK!'

Ideas

– Acting out. Encourage children to experiment with different voices, for example, a sweet voice as well as an angry voice.
– Topic: monkeys—where they live, what they eat, stories about monkeys.
– Topic: bananas—where they come from, how they are grown and transported. Many of the bananas bought in Europe come from the West Indies. They are picked when they are green and then ripen in the ship on the way to Europe.

6.2 The parrot

Narrator: 'Helen has got a parrot.'
Helen: 'Say, "Pretty Polly".'

Helen: 'No, say, "Pretty Polly" and don't say, "Say, Pretty Polly".'
Parrot: 'No, say, "Pretty Polly" and don't say, "Say, Pretty Polly".'
Helen: 'No!'
Parrot: 'No!'
Helen: 'You are a stupid parrot!'
Parrot: 'You are a stupid girl!'

Ideas

- This mini play invites acting out! The success of the performance lies in the ability of Helen to represent patience, impatience, exasperation, anger, etc.
- It would be very amusing to write alternative 'Helen and Parrot' dialogues.

6.3 The two little kittens

There are two little kittens in the middle of a big wood. It is the middle of the night. It is twelve o'clock. The two little kittens are frightened.

There are twelve big wolves. The twelve big wolves are coming. The two little kittens are going. The twelve big wolves are walking. The two little kittens are walking. The twelve big wolves are running. The two little kittens are running. The two little kittens are swimming. The twelve big wolves are swimming.

The two little kittens are flying. The twelve big wolves can't fly!

Ideas

- Help the class to make up their own story by asking: *Who do you want in your story? Where are they? What time is it? What happens?*
- This story invites dramatization! The quietest version is for the children to remain seated. A noisier version would be for the children to act the part of the kittens and the wolves and to move in a clear space in the classroom or school hall.
- Your children could take the pattern of the story and substitute other animals, places, times, and actions.

1 This story was made up by a class of children from Premontrei Primary School, Gödöllö, Hungary. The children were aged ten and had done about three months of English. The only word I supplied was the word 'frightened'. If you tell this story to your children, tell them it was made up by Hungarian children.

2 Techniques for storymaking with children are described at greater length in the companion volume to this book, *Creating Stories with Children*.

Elementary

6.4 The donkey and the little dog

A man has a donkey and a little dog.

The donkey lives in a warm, clean stable and it has hay and water. The little dog lives in the house. It sits on the man's knees in the evening and sleeps in a chair in front of the fire in the night. It eats good meat and biscuits, and the man gives it food from the table.

'It's not fair!' says the donkey. 'I want to live in the house.'

One day the donkey leaves the stable and goes into the house. It plays in the house. It breaks the furniture and the glasses and the cups and the plates. It sits on the man's knee!

'Get out of the house!' shouts the man. 'You have got a nice stable!'

What is good for a little dog may not be good for a donkey.

Ideas

This is another story about an animal wanting to live where it is inappropriate, plus the funny things that happen.

- Acting out
- Some children describe habitats; other children have to guess which animal lives there. Examples:
  high trees, jungle = monkeys
  river, swamp = crocodile
  woods, gardens, fields, and farms = fox
  cushion, bed, kitchen, garden = cat

6.5 Who is my friend?

Two boys, Frank and Joe, are walking along a road. They are friends.

They talk and they laugh.
They see a big boy. He is fishing.

Frank says, 'Hey Joe! Shout, "You are stupid! You catch old boots, you can't catch fish!" '
'No, I don't want to,' says Joe.
'Go on, Joe! Go on!'

Joe shouts, 'Hey! You catch old boots! You can't catch fish in a million years!'
The big boy stands up. 'What?'
Frank says, 'Let's go!' He begins to run.
Joe runs but he falls. He hurts his leg. 'Frank, help!'
Frank shouts, 'No way!' And he runs away.

The big boy comes. He says, 'Are you OK?'
'It's my leg!' says Joe.
'Here, hold my arm,' says the big boy. 'My name's Mark.'
They walk to the river, to Mark's chair.
'Sit down here. Hold the rod!'

The next day, Frank and Joe meet at school.
'Hi!'
'Hi!'
'Are you OK?'
'Yes.'
'What are you doing tonight?'
'Fishing.'
'Fishing? Who with?'
'Mark.'
'Mark? Who's he?'
'Oh, he's a friend.'

Ideas

– List the important things in a friend. First, all the class brainstorm words and phrases on the board which describe people. Examples: strong, handsome, rich, intelligent, funny, kind, he helps people, etc. Then each child makes his or her own list, putting the words in order from important to not important. They discuss their choices in groups of four.
– The children rewrite the story with five changes. They read it out to their neighbour. The neighbour tries to identify which bits have been changed.
– Make a video or audio tape of the story.
– The children retell the story but substitute new names and actions. (See also 6.16, 'The travellers and the bear'.)

6.6 The boy who cried wolf

A shepherd boy was looking after his sheep on the mountain. He was bored so he shouted, 'Help! Wolf!'

Then he watched all the people run up the mountain from the town.
He laughed.
'Where's the wolf? Where's the wolf?' the people asked.
'It ran away!' the boy said.

Next day he was bored so he shouted, 'Help! Wolf!'
Then he watched all the people run up the mountain from the town.
He laughed.
'Where's the wolf? Where's the wolf?' the people asked.
'It ran away!' the boy said.

On the third day a wolf came so he shouted, 'Help! Wolf!'
The people in the town heard him but they said, 'It's not true. He's bored. He wants to see us run up the mountain.'
So the wolf ate the sheep and the boy.

Ideas

- When you have told the story once or twice, ask one child to be the boy, one the wolf, about ten the sheep, and about ten the people. Retell the story with the children playing their parts.
- Jump up word. Give each child one or two words from the story. Every time they hear their words they jump up and sit down. Let them exchange words after one or two readings so that they can jump up and sit down for different ones.
- Whistling story. Tell the story but whistle instead of saying some of the words. See if the children can guess the missing words.
- Discuss the moral of the story and ask the children to give other examples.

6.7 The fox and the crow

A crow sits in a tree. The crow has a big piece of cheese in its beak.

A fox comes and sees the crow and the cheese.
'What a beautiful bird! What beautiful eyes! What beautiful feathers! Has she got a beautiful voice? I don't know!'

The crow opens her mouth and says, 'Caw!' The big piece of cheese falls down. The fox eats it! Then the fox says, 'She hasn't got a beautiful voice and she hasn't got any brains!'

Be careful of tricky people.

Ideas

- Tell the class that the trees can speak as well. Brainstorm with the class what the trees might say during this story. Agree on some simple sentences, and write them on the board, for example:

> Crow, crow, eat your cheese!
> Crow, crow, don't listen to the fox, don't listen to the fox!
> Fox, fox, go away, go away!
> Fox, fox, you're not kind, you're not kind.
> Stupid bird, stupid bird!

Act out the story using three children: one for the narrator, one for the fox, and one for the crow. The other children can be trees and whisper their commentary as if it is a breeze through their branches.

6.8 Ghosts

A man lives in an old house. One evening he is reading a book.

He puts his glasses on the table.
The first ghost takes the glasses.
The man says, 'Where are my glasses?'
He looks for them but he can't find them.

He puts his apple on the table.
The second ghost takes the apple.
The man says, 'Where is my apple?'
He looks for his apple but he can't find it.

He puts his book on the table.
The third ghost takes the book.
The man says, 'Where is my book?'
He looks for his book but he can't find it.

It is midnight. The man goes to sleep. He snores very loudly.
The ghosts don't like his snoring. They run out of the house.
They leave his glasses, his apple, and his book on the table.

Ideas

- The form of this story invites 'listen and act' and would be an amusing video for the children to make. Note that even a child can make a big snoring noise by snoring into a large tin can.
- The children could add extra things for the ghosts to steal.
- We don't know what the man, the house, or the ghosts look like, nor what season it is, what the weather is like, nor where the house is. Discuss this with the class. You could make a big picture together.
- The children can produce a ghost book with one page from each child with his or her own invention of what the ghosts

could do to frighten the man. Here is a possible ghost shape for the book, with the pages and cover cut to shape:

- In pairs, the children draw their idea of a ghost and write about where it is and what it does to frighten or annoy people. The drawings can be displayed on the wall.

Pre-intermediate

6.9 The skiing accident

I like skiing but I am not very good. Once, I went to the top of a mountain on a ski lift. It was foggy. I couldn't see very well. The snow was very icy and hard. It was too difficult for me so I decided to slalom very slowly. I ski'd from side to side.

Then some friends came. They stopped and waited for me. I told them I was frightened and they laughed and said, 'Follow us. You will be OK.'

So I followed them into the fog and we went very fast. Suddenly they turned to the right but I couldn't! I ski'd straight on! I went up a little hill, and then flew through the air, and then began to fall! I was very, very lucky! I fell into the branches of a tree. The branches were covered with snow. I lay on the top branches in the snow and I didn't fall off! I lay still; I didn't move.

My friends came to look for me. I waited for about half an hour and then they saw me in the tree! They came to the bottom of the tree and one of them climbed up and then reached out for me. He took my hand. I was safe!

Ideas

- Tell the children the story and ask them to tell you if they think it is a true story. In fact it is not a true story although my own skiing skills made me imagine that it could happen to me one day if I am not careful.
- Ask the children if they would like to invent their own amazing story. Do this as a whole-class activity—it would be difficult for children to do it by themselves. This type of story is called a 'tall tale'.

6.10 The kangaroo in the jacket

A family from Manchester went to Australia on holiday. They hired a car for one month and drove up the east coast and into the desert. In Australia you must be very careful because kangaroos sometimes jump across the road.

The family were driving along through the desert when a kangaroo jumped in front of them. The car hit the kangaroo and it went over the roof.

The family stopped their car and went back to look at the kangaroo. It was lying on the road.

The man wanted to be funny. He took off his jacket and put it on the kangaroo! Then he picked up the kangaroo and said to his wife: 'Quick! Take a photograph!'

But the kangaroo wasn't dead! It was only unconscious and when the man picked it up it woke up again. It opened its eyes and then jumped away across the desert! It was wearing the man's jacket! And the man had his spectacles, his car keys, his money, and his passport in the jacket! And they never saw the kangaroo again!

Ideas

This type of story is called a 'modern myth' or an 'urban legend'. People tell these stories as if they are true, but nobody knows if they are true or not!

- Ask the children if they think it is true.

- Ask the children to work in pairs and to try and retell the story so that the story becomes theirs. Then they can tell it later at home.

6.11 Jogger in New York

There was this man in New York. He jogged into Central Park every morning. He always took a five-dollar bill with him in his top pocket. He jogged into the park and went to the café by the lake. He always bought himself a coffee and a doughnut.

One day he jogged into the park and another jogger knocked into him. For few moments he didn't think about it, then he suddenly thought, 'Hey! this guy might be a pickpocket!' He felt for his five-dollar bill in his pocket. It wasn't there! The other guy had taken it!

He thought, 'There is too much crime in New York! I always say honest people must fight crime!'
The other jogger was only 30 metres ahead. The first jogger ran after him, hit him on the shoulder, and said, 'Give us the money!' The second jogger said, 'OK! Just stay cool! Take it easy! Take it easy!'
Then the second jogger gave the first jogger a five-dollar bill. The second jogger then ran away as fast as he could!

The first jogger ran to the café. He felt really good. He had fought crime. He had got his money back again. He bought himself a coffee and *two* doughnuts.

Then he ran home. His wife was waiting. She was shaking her head. 'Oh dear! Oh dear!' she said. 'You've had a bad morning, haven't you?'
'No! Why? I've had a very good morning!' he said.
'Really?' she said. 'But you left your five-dollar bill on the table!'

Ideas

This is another of those urban myths or modern legends (see 6.10, 'The kangaroo in the jacket'). People tell this type of story and say it is true.

- It's a good story. Ask the children to try to tell it to each other until they can all do so.
- Compare it with the story of Gellert (6.12) in which a prince, many years ago, also jumped to conclusions, took action, and then found he was wrong.
- Discuss with the children in their mother tongue the way in which we often think we understand a situation and think someone has done wrong to us and even take action. Later we find we are wrong. It happens every day in school.

– Topic: USA and New York—perceptions from television; history and geography.

6.12 Gellert

There was a prince; his name was Llewellyn. His uncle, King John, gave him a dog, a hunting dog. The dog's name was Gellert. Gellert was a fine hunting dog. When he left the castle he could smell a deer one kilometre away. He could run faster than a deer. He was so strong that he could knock a deer over. He was a fine hunting dog.

One day Prince Llewellyn went hunting with his friends. He called all his dogs. But Gellert wouldn't go. Gellert stood in the doorway of the castle and wagged his tail and put his head on one side, but he would not leave the castle.

Llewellyn was angry! He shouted, 'Come on, Gellert! Come here!' But Gellert wouldn't leave the castle. So Llewellyn and his friends went hunting with the other dogs.

Llewellyn and his friends caught nothing. When they came back to the castle they were angry. As they came to the castle Gellert bounded out towards them, wagging his tail. As he came closer Llewellyn saw there was blood on Gellert's face and sides.

'How could that be?' Llewellyn thought. 'Gellert sometimes plays with my child. Gellert is half wolf, half wild. Perhaps he has killed my child!' And Llewellyn ran into the castle. He ran to the child's room. All the furniture was turned over. There was blood everywhere. Llewellyn couldn't see his child.

Prince Llewellyn took his sword and drove it into the side of Gellert. With the last gasp for life of Gellert, Llewellyn heard the cry of his child from beneath the overturned cot. Llewellyn ran to the cot, turned it over, and there was the child, perfectly safe, perfectly well. But behind the cot was a dead wolf.

Llewellyn was very sad. What could he do? He couldn't bring Gellert back to life! He dug a hole for Gellert outside the castle. He put Gellert in the hole and covered him with stones, a great pile of stones. He put a plaque on the stones: 'To Gellert, a faithful dog.'

You can still see this pile of stones in North Wales. The place is called Beddgellert, 'the grave of Gellert' in the Welsh language.

Ideas

This is a very moving story but it is an important one for children. Many of them have been accused wrongly and have themselves accused others wrongly. We do it every day.

- Compare this story to 6.11, 'Jogger in New York', a modern story based on the same kind of misunderstanding.
- Ask the children to try to tell the story to their neighbours in order to learn it. They may have to do this in their mother tongue.
- Ask groups of children each to make a book of the story with each child writing, designing, and illustrating two pages.
- Topic: Wales—landscape, music, language, history, industry.
- Topic: Dogs—types, behaviour, uses, 'man's best friend'.

6.13 Oh no, I'm a cat!

It was a warm summer's day. David and Maggie, his sister, were in the garden. Maggie wanted to read her book, but David wanted to talk.
'That cat is amazing! Look! It walks beautifully!'
'Be quiet. I'm reading. I'm going to be a TV star.'
'Watch me. I'm a cat! I'm going to jump on that wall.'
'Be careful! That's the one-eyed man's wall. He can see you!'

David walked along the wall. The one-eyed man didn't see him. But something started to happen to David . . .
'You've got hairs on your hands!'
'I feel ill!'
'You're getting smaller! You've got hairs on your face! You're horrible! Urrhhh!'
'I'm changing into a cat! Help me, Maggie!'
'What can I do?'

David changed into a cat! He was very unhappy.
'Tell Mum and Dad! Quick! Help! HEL . . . IAOW!'
'You're a cat!'
'Miaow!'
'Can you understand me?'
'Miaow!'
'Say "Miaow" five times.'
'Miaow. Miaow. Miaow. Miaow. Miaow.'

Maggie was very pleased. She had a clever cat. She wanted to be a rich and famous TV star.
'David, you are a wonderful cat. We can go on television. We are going to be rich and famous.'
'Miaow!'
'Now, let's practise. Lift your right paw!'
'Miaow!'
'Jump ten times!'
'Miaow!'
'David, jump ten times! OK! I'm going to tell Mum. You're a horrible cat! You can't live in this house if you're not nice.'

Maggie was very happy and excited! David was hungry; he saw
Gilbert, Maggie's canary. Its door was open.
'Hello, Gilbert. How is my little Gilbert?'
'Miaow!'
'David, stop it! Leave Gilbert alone!'
'Tweet! Tweet!'
'Poor Gilbert! Gilbert! David, you are a stupid cat! You horrible,
stupid cat! Get out of the house!'

David's parents came home. David was very pleased. He
miaowed and he rubbed against their legs. He was their son, and
he wanted his mum and dad to know.
'Oh look, there's a cat!'
'Miaow!'
'What a nice little cat!'
'Miaow! Miaow!'
'All right, get down now. You must go home. Go home to
mummy!'
'Go on! Shoo! Go away! Go home!'

Ideas

This story is the first part of my own story, *Oh no, I'm a cat!*,
from the Spellbinders series published by Oxford University
Press.

- Ask the children to think of an ending and then to compare
  theirs with the one that I wrote. Please emphasize to the
  children that my ending is not the 'correct' ending and may
  not be better than theirs! Let each child decide which is the
  best ending for him or her. By all means find the ending
  which the majority prefer.
- Ask who has a cat. Would they like to be one? What else
  might they turn into? What are the advantages and
  disadvantages? This can lead to mime, guessing games, etc.
- Topic: cats.

6.14 The wise shoemaker

There was a shoemaker in a village in Hungary. His name was
Yosser. Yosser was a good shoemaker but he was also very wise.
People came to his shop with their problems as well as their
shoes!

Sometimes mothers came and asked, 'What can I do with my
son? He is so lazy!'
Sometimes farmers came and asked, 'What can I do with my
farm? I have no money and I cannot buy any corn!'
Yosser always gave good advice. More and more people came to
him. He hardly had time to make any shoes! Rich people came

to see him. They travelled for a day to get to his village. They just wanted to get his advice.

Now one day, a rich man in Budapest wanted to have a wonderful wedding for his daughter. He wanted the wedding to be famous. Of course, he invited the best cooks to make wonderful food. And, of course, he invited the best musicians to make wonderful music. But everybody has good cooks and musicians. Then he got an idea! He decided to invite Yosser, the wise shoemaker! 'Yosser will come to the wedding and then the wedding will be famous!' So the rich man invited Yosser. Yosser was very pleased! He wanted to go to Budapest! It was his first time in a big city!

Yosser arrived in Budapest. It was raining and the streets were full of holes and the holes were full of water. Yosser looked at the big houses and fell into a hole full of water and mud! He got out of the hole but he was wet and dirty. He ran to the house of the rich man. The servants opened the door and saw Yosser. They said, 'Go away! No beggars today! It is the daughter's wedding and it is going to be a famous wedding!' And they threw Yosser into another hole!

Now, Yosser knew another rich man in Budapest. Yosser went to his house. He washed himself and he borrowed some fine clothes from the other rich man. He borrowed some high, soft, brown leather boots; a pair of soft, white woollen trousers; a white silken shirt; and a green coat with golden buttons. Then he went to the house of the wedding. Everybody was happy to see Yosser!
'You must have the best seat at the wedding!' said the rich man. 'You must sit next to the bride and groom!'

Yosser stood and held up his glass of wine. 'Your good health!' he said, and then he poured the wine into the pocket of his green coat with the golden buttons. People were amazed! But Yosser laughed and sat down.

Then the soup came. Yosser took off his boots and poured the soup into them. People were amazed but Yosser laughed and put his boots back on again.

The meat and potatoes and vegetables came. Yosser took the meat and put it into the pocket of his trousers and then he rubbed the vegetables into his white silken shirt. People were amazed but Yosser laughed.

Suddenly the rich man shouted, 'Are you crazy? Are you a wise man or a fool?'

Yosser said, 'Oh, I'm sorry! You see, I came twice this morning. The first time your servants threw me into a hole and the second time you said, "Welcome!" The only difference was my clothes! So I thought you had invited my clothes to dinner! So I fed my clothes!'

Ideas

- The children draw a picture of their favourite part of the story and write one or two sentences under the picture.
- The children think of problems and ask each other for advice. They reply using *Why don't you . . . ?* and *You should . . . .*
- The children write a postcard or a letter from Yosser to his family.
- The children write a page of Yosser's journal about his visit to Budapest.

6.15 The cat, the cock, and the young mouse

A young mouse said to his mother, 'I saw a cat and a cock today. The cat was very nice. She was soft and gentle and kind, and had beautiful eyes. The cock was horrible. It was a monster! It had long strong legs with big claws and it had a big beak and suddenly it made a horrible noise! I was frightened!'

The mother mouse said, 'The cat wants to eat you. The cock doesn't!'

A nice face may hide a nasty mind.

Ideas

- Rewrite alternative versions of the same moral.

6.16 The travellers and the bear

Two men were walking in a forest. Suddenly a bear came. One man ran and climbed up a tree. The other man couldn't run and couldn't fight the bear by himself so he lay on the ground. The bear came to the man and sniffed at his head. Then the bear went away.

'What did the bear say?' said the man in the tree.
The man on the ground said, 'The bear said, "Is he your friend? Why did he leave you?"'

Bad luck tests friendship.

Ideas

- The children can mime this story as you tell it. You can actually manipulate the children, using them almost like puppets (pulling them, pushing them and generally directing them) to mime what you are saying.

- What is a good friend? The children brainstorm and list all the things they think are important.
- Compare this story with others in the book or others you know. See 6.5, 'Who is my friend?', page 193.
- The children invent and maybe write another fable to show what friendship is for them.

6.17 The wind and the sun

The wind and the sun argued.
The wind said, 'I'm stronger than you!'
The sun said, 'No, I'm stronger than you!'

They saw a traveller. He was walking on the road.
'I can take off his coat!' said the wind. And he blew and he blew and he blew. But the wind couldn't take off the man's coat.

'I can take off his coat!' said the sun. And the sun warmed the man. The man became hot and he took off his coat.

Kindness is stronger than violence.

Ideas

- This is obviously a nice story for illustrating comparatives and past tense forms.
- Invite the children to make silly boasts, for example:
  I am stronger/faster/cleverer than you.
  I can run faster than you.
  I can run at one million miles an hour.
- Topic: weather.
- This story lends itself to being acted out. A lot of children can play the parts of the sun and the wind. There can be several travellers.
- The children can chorus the rival claims of the wind and the sun in two groups.

7 Pages to copy

How to draw people

Stick people

elbows half way

hips half way

knees half way

Solid people

First draw a box for the body.
Then draw stick arms and legs.
Then draw the thickness of the arms and legs.

208

king	queen	prince	princess
lady	soldier	jester	cook
baby	witch	wizard	dwarf
giant	dragon	monster	ghost
beggar	Megaman	Robin Hood	pirate

How to draw animals
Choose: ☐ ☐ ○ ○ △ ▷ etc.

Then add details

bear

bird

cat

dog

eagle

elephant

fish

fox

210

frog	goat	goose	hedgehog
horse	kangaroo	lion	monkey
mouse	parrot	pig	rabbit
shark	sheep	snake	swan
tiger	tortoise	whale	wolf

Places and things

boat	bridge	bus	car
castle	cave	cottage	fire
forest	house	mountain	palace
plane	planet	river	spaceship
tent	town	village	volcano

Further reading

Teachers' resources

Aurilia, S. 1994. 'Using a story children already know in their mother tongue in the English class' in D. Hill (ed.): *Changing Contexts in English Language Teaching*. Italy: The British Council, 1994.

Barton, B. 1986. *Tell me Another: Storytelling and Reading Aloud at Home, at School and in the Community*. Markham, Ontario: Pembroke Publishers.

Barton, B. and **D. Booth**. 1990. *Stories in the Classroom*. Markham, Ontario: Pembroke Publishers. A very useful book.

Bettelheim, B. 1991. *The Uses of Enchantment: The Meaning and Importance of Fairy Tales*. Harmondsworth: Penguin. This book concentrates on what fairy stories might be offering our children beneath the surface level of entertainment. An important book.

Colwell, E. 1991 (new edn). *Storytelling*. Stroud, UK: Thimble Press. A useful book from a great storyteller.

Corbett, P. and **B. Moses**. 1991. *My Grandmother's Motor Bike: Story Writing in the Primary School*. Oxford: Oxford University Press. A wonderful source of rich ideas.

Cross, J. et al. *Long Ago and Far Away*. Birmingham: Birmingham Development Education Centre. Links storytelling techniques with history and geography and explores themes such as families and bereavement.

Dufeu, B. 1994. *Teaching Myself*. Oxford: Oxford University Press. Explores the use of myths and fairy tales in language teaching.

Ellis, G. and **J. Brewster**. 1991. *The Storytelling Handbook for Primary Teachers*. Harmondsworth: Penguin. A useful book for relating storybooks to the whole curriculum.

Emblen, V. and **H. Schmitz**. 1991. *Bright Ideas: Learning Through Story*. Leamington Spa: Scholastic Publications. A useful source of ideas on using stories in class, with a good address list and Further Reading section.

Garvie, E. 1990. *Story as Vehicle*. Clevedon/Philadelphia: Multilingual Matters. Sets stories into a framework for language teaching.

Handler, A.I. 1993. *The English Storyteller*. Israel: University Publishing Projects Ltd. A collection of stories plus video and workbook.

Howe, A. and **J. Johnson**. 1992. *Common Bonds: Storytelling in the Classroom.* London: Hodder and Stoughton. A very useful book.

Johnson, K. 1989. *Impro.* London: Routledge, Chapman, and Hall. An inspired book on digging out the creativity in all of us.

Morgan, J. and **M. Rinvolucri**. 1983. *Once Upon a Time.* Cambridge: Cambridge University Press. This was the first book in the field of using stories in foreign language teaching and is excellent.

Phillips, S. 1993. *Young Learners.* Resource books for Teachers series. Oxford: Oxford University Press. Lots of ideas and advice for teaching English to children aged 6 to 12.

Ralston, M.V. 1993. *An Exchange of Gifts.* Pippin Teachers' Library. Oxford: Heinemann. Half the book is Further Reading, which is useful.

Rosen, B. 1988. *And None of It was Nonsense.* London: Mary Glasgow Publications. The author has done a lot of excellent work with inner-city teenagers.

Rosen, B. 1993 (new edn). *Shapers and Polishers.* London: Mary Glasgow Publications. A rich resource.

Rosen, M. 1989. *Did I Hear you Write?* London: André Deutsch. A very good writer and storyteller who gets people to listen to themselves.

Sylvester, R. et al. 1991. *Start with a Story.* Birmingham: Birmingham Development Education Centre. Suggests how stories can be used for exploring children's concerns, feelings, experiences, and issues.

Watts, I.N. 1992. *Making Stories.* Markham, Ontario: Pembroke Publishers. A very good book, particularly for helping children to make stories themselves.

Wheway, D. and **S. Thomson**. 1993. *Explore Music through Stories.* Oxford: Oxford University Press. Ideas for eleven stories including 'Goldilocks' and 'The Wind and the Sun'.

Wray, D. 1987. *Bright Ideas Writing.* Leamington Spa: Scholastic Publications. Lots of practical ideas. One book in an excellent series.

Wright, A. 1984. *Games for Language Learning.* Cambridge: Cambridge University Press. A large collection of games and activities for language teaching, many of which are useful in presenting and practising language items before a story is told. There is also a section of ideas for story making and writing.

Wright, A. 1989. *Pictures for Language Learning.* Cambridge: Cambridge University Press. Over 350 ways of using magazine pictures and simple drawings, many of them for storytelling and writing.

Wright, A. 1994 (2nd edn). *1000 + Pictures for Teachers to Copy.* London: Nelson. More than 1000 pictures of everyday objects, people, animals, and situations for teachers to copy by hand or photocopy. Based on wide experience of teachers' needs.

Wright, A. In preparation. *Creating Stories with Children.*
Oxford: Oxford University Press. Resource Books for Teachers
series. The companion book to this one, with much more on
helping children to make their own stories and books.

Wright, A. and **S. Haleem.** 1991. *Visuals for the Language
Classroom.* Harlow: Longman. Practical ideas for using all the
media in the classroom creatively including story making and
writing.

Stories

Ahlberg, A. and **J. Ahlberg.** 1980. *Funnybones.* Oxford:
Heinemann. Starts with the 'Dark, dark town' and goes on to
a series of stories about a family of skeletons.

Cole, B. 1987. *The Slimy Book.* London: Armada Picture Lions.
Plenty of repetition, getting ever more ridiculous until it all
turns out to have been a dream.

Dahl, R. 1984. *Revolting Rhymes.* Harmondsworth: Penguin.
Shows how traditional tales can be adapted.

French, F. 1986. *Snow White in New York.* Oxford: Oxford
University Press. An adaptation of *Snow White,* highly
acclaimed, recommended for reading in British primary
schools.

Hallworth, G. 1992. *Cric Crac.* London: Mammoth.

Hallworth, G. 1992. *Listen to This Story.* London: Mammoth.
Two collections of short West Indian stories. The second book
is aimed at older children and is slightly more complicated.

Handford, M. 1987. *Where's Wally?* London: Walker Books.

Handford, M. 1988. *Where's Wally Now?* London: Walker
Books.

Handford, M. 1989. *Where's Wally: The Fantastic Journey.*
London: Walker Books. These have become cult classics for 7-
to 12-year-olds. Although they do not contain a lot of writing,
they are a rich source of language work and can be used as a
springboard to topic work.

Nicoll, H. and **J. Pienkowski.** 1975. *Meg and Mog* books.
Harmondsworth: Penguin. Simple but zany pictures and
stories about a witch, her cat, and an owl.

Paul, K. and **P. Carter.** 1989. *Captain Teachum's Buried
Treasure.* Oxford: Oxford University Press. Good for practising
prepositions and 'where'.

Ramanujan, A.K. 1992. *Folktales from India.* New York:
Pantheon.

Rosen, M. (ed.). 1992. *South, North, East, and West.* London:
Walker Books/Oxford: Oxfam. A collection of 25 stories from
around the world. Many of the stories are meant to be told
aloud.

Sendak, M. 1964 (latest edition 1993). *Where the Wild Things Are*. London: HarperCollins. This book has many levels and should appeal to age groups from 4 to 11.

Smith, A.M. 1989. *Children of Wax: African Folk Tales*. Edinburgh: Canongate. Includes 'Strange animal'.

Tolstoy, A. and **H. Oxenbury.** *The Great Big Enormous Turnip*. Oxford: Heinemann. Many teachers recommend this. It is also available in ELT adaptations from Collins ELT and Ladybird.

Trivizas, E. 1993. *The Three Little Wolves and the Big Bad Pig*. Oxford: Heinemann. Turns the story on its head—a fun way to make it appeal to older children.

Webb, K. (ed.). 1986. *I Like This Story: A Taste of 50 Favourites*. Harmondsworth: Penguin. Highlights from 50 excellent books which will whet children's appetites.

Williamson, D. 1987. *Tell Me a Story for Christmas*. Edinburgh: Canongate.

Williamson, D. 1993. *Fireside Tales of the Traveller Children*. Edinburgh: Canongate.

Williamson, D. 1995. *How the Rabbit Lost His Tail*. Cambridge: Cambridge University Press.

Wright, A. 1900. *Nessy*. Nelson Storychest series. Walton-on-Thames: Nelson.

There are also several books which have been translated into many languages or are available in dual-language editions. These include many well-known ones such as:

Carle, E. 1984. *The Very Hungry Caterpillar*. Harmondsworth: Penguin.

Hill, E. 1980. *Where's Spot?* Harmondsworth: Penguin.

McKee, D. 1990. *Elmer: The Story of a Patchwork Elephant*. London: Red Fox.

ELT readers/adaptations

Many publishers have series of books adapted for learners of all ages and levels. For example:

Heinemann Children's Readers
Longman Easy Starts
Penguin Ready Readers
Oxford University Press Bookworms: for older children.
Oxford University Press Classic Tales: fairy stories such as *Cinderella, Goldilocks,* and *Little Red Riding Hood.*
Favourite Fairy Tales Series, Longman. Books and videos of the most famous of Hans Christian Andersen's fairy tales.

Briggs, R. and **G. Ellis.** 1995. *The Snowman*. Oxford: Oxford University Press. The classic story retold for learners of English with activities, teachers' notes, and cassette.

Paul, K. and **Thomas, V.** 1995. *Winnie the Witch*. Oxford:

Oxford University Press. A simplified version of an award-winning children's book, with activities, teachers' notes, and cassette.

Wright, A. 'Spellbinders' series. Oxford: Oxford University Press. A series of six original stories at three levels, with exercises. Particularly suitable for dramatizing.

Index to activities

Language points

All the activities practise the skill of listening.

Topics and cross-curricular work

Other titles in the Resource Books for Teachers series

Beginners, by Peter Grundy—over 100 original and communicative activities for teaching both absolute and 'false' beginners. Includes a section for learners who do not know the Latin alphabet. (ISBN 0 19 437200 6)

CALL, by David Hardisty and Scott Windeatt—a bank of practical activities, based on communicative methodology, which make use of a variety of computer programs. (ISBN 0 19 437105 0)

Class Readers, by Jean Greenwood—practical advice and activities to develop extensive and intensive reading skills, listening activities, oral tasks, and perceptive skills. (ISBN 0 19 437103 4)

Classroom Dynamics, by Jill Hadfield—a practical book to help teachers maintain a good working relationship with their classes, and so promote effective learning. (ISBN 0 19 437147 8)

Conversation, by Rob Nolasco and Lois Arthur—more than 80 activities which develop students' ability to speak confidently and fluently. (ISBN 0 19 437096 8)

Cultural Awareness, by Barry Tomalin and Susan Stempleski—activities to challenge stereotypes, using cultural issues as a rich resource for language practice. (ISBN 0 19 437194 8)

Drama, by Charlyn Wessels—first-hand, practical advice on using drama to teach spoken communication skills and literature, and to make language learning more creative and enjoyable. (ISBN 0 19 437097 6)

Grammar Dictation, by Ruth Wajnryb—also known as 'dictogloss', this technique improves students' understanding and use of grammar by reconstructing texts to find out more about how English works. (ISBN 0 19 437004 6)

Learner-based Teaching, by Colin Campbell and Hanna Kryszewska—over 70 language practice activities which unlock the wealth of knowledge that learners bring to the classroom. (ISBN 0 19 437163 8)

Literature, by Alan Maley and Alan Duff—an innovatory book on using literature for language practice. (ISBN 0 19 437094 1)

Music and Song, by Tim Murphey—shows teachers how 'tuning in' to their students' musical tastes can increase motivation and tap a rich vein of resources. (ISBN 0 19 437055 0)

Newspapers, by Peter Grundy—creative and original ideas for making effective use of newspapers in lessons. (ISBN 0 19 437192 6)

Project Work, by Diana L. Fried-Booth—practical resources for teachers who are interested in bridging the gap between the classroom and the outside world. (ISBN 0 19 437092 5)

Pronunciation, by Clement Laroy—imaginative activities to build confidence and improve all aspects of pronunciation. (ISBN 0 19 437089 0)

Role Play, by Gillian Porter Ladousse—from highly controlled conversations to improvised drama, and from simple dialogues to complex scenarios. (ISBN 0 19 437095 X)

Self-Access, by Susan Sheerin—helps teachers with the practicalities of setting up and managing self-access study facilities to enable learning to continue independently of teaching. (ISBN 0 19 437099 2)

Translation, by Alan Duff—provides a wide variety of translation activities from many different subject areas. (ISBN 0 19 437104 2)

Video, by Richard Cooper, Mike Lavery, and Mario Rinvolucri—video watching and making tasks involving the language of perception, observation, and argumentation. (ISBN 0 19 437192 6)

Vocabulary, by John Morgan and Mario Rinvolucri—a wide variety of communicative activities for teaching new words to learners of any foreign language. (ISBN 0 19 437091 7)

Writing, by Tricia Hedge—presents a wide range of writing tasks to improve learners' 'authoring' and 'crafting' skills, as well as guidance on student difficulties with writing. (ISBN 0 19 437098 4)

Young Learners, by Sarah Phillips—advice, ideas, and materials for a wide variety of language practice activities, including arts and crafts, games, storytelling, poems, and songs. (ISBN 0 19 437195 6)